Post-Secondary Education: Preparation for the World of Work

The Institute for Research on Public Policy
L'Institut de recherches politiques

A national, independent, research organization
Un organisme de recherche national et indépendant

Créé en 1972, l'Institut de recherches politiques est un organisme national dont l'indépendance et l'autonomie sont assurées grâce aux revenus provenant d'un fonds de dotation auquel souscrivent les gouvernements fédéral et provinciaux ainsi que le secteur privé. L'Institut obtient en outre des subventions et des contrats des gouvernements, des compagnies et des fondations afin de réaliser certains projets de recherche.

La raison d'être de l'Institut est triple :

- Servir de catalyseur au sein de la collectivité nationale en favorisant un débat public éclairé sur les principales questions d'intérêt général.
- Stimuler la participation de tous les éléments de la collectivité nationale à l'élaboration de la politique d'État.
- Trouver des solutions réalisables aux importants problèmes d'ordre politique afin de contribuer à l'élaboration d'une saine politique d'État.

Un Conseil d'administration, chargé de la décision, et une Commission de direction, responsable d'éclairer le Conseil sur l'orientation de la recherche, assurent la direction de l'Institut. L'administration courante des politiques, des programmes et du personnel relève du président.

L'Institut fonctionne de manière décentralisée et retient les services de chercheurs en divers points du Canada, s'assurant ainsi que toutes les régions contribuent aux recherches.

L'Institut cherche à favoriser, dans la mesure du possible, la compréhension et la discussion publiques des questions d'envergure nationale, controversées ou non. Il publie les conclusions de ses recherches avec clarté et impartialité. Les recommandations ou les conclusions énoncées dans les publications de l'Institut sont strictement celles de l'auteur et n'engagent aucunement le Conseil d'administration, la Commission de direction ou les bailleurs de fonds.

Le président assume la responsabilité ultime de publier un manuscrit au nom de l'Institut. Il jouit à cette fin des conseils du personnel de l'Institut et de critiques de l'extérieur quant à l'exactitude et à l'objectivité du texte. Ne sont publiés que les textes qui traitent de façon compétente d'un sujet digne de la réflexion du public.

Post-Secondary Education: Preparation for the World of Work

Proceedings of a Canada/UK Colloquium
November 21-22, 1988
Mississauga, Ontario
Canada

Edited by
Ron Watts and
Jeff Greenberg

Ministry of Education, Ontario
Information Services & Resources Unit,
13th Floor, Mowat Block, Queen's Park,
Toronto M7A 1L2

The Institute for Research on Public Policy
L'Institut de recherches politiques

Dartmouth
Aldershot · Brookfield USA · Hong Kong · Singapore · Sydney

Copyright © The Institute for Research on Public Policy 1990

All rights reserved.

Published by

Dartmouth Publishing Company Limited
Gower House, Croft Road
Aldershot, Hants GU11 3HR
England

ISBN 1 85521 062 2

The Institute for Research on Public Policy
P.O. Box 3670 South
Halifax, Nova Scotia
Canada
B3J 3K6

ISBN 0-88645-091-8

British Library Cataloguing in Publication Data
Post-secondary education : preparation for the world
  of work : proceedings of a Canada/UK colloquium,
  November 21-22 1988, Mississauga, Ontario, Canada.
  1. Developed countries. Vocational education &
  training
  I. Watts, Ron   II. Greenberg, Jeff
  370.11'3'091722

Printed in Great Britain by
Athenaeum Press Ltd, Newcastle upon Tyne.

Contents

Preface ix

Préface xiii

Introduction 1
    Ronald L. Watts

Colloquium Papers

I.   **The Challenge of Change** 9

    The Challenge of Change for 2001: The Canadian
    University in a Knowledge-Intensive Society 11
        Geraldine A. Kenny-Wallace

    Education, Economic Prosperity and the Role of the
    State: Britain's Problem in Perspective 25
        John Rae

II. Coordination versus Decentralisation 35

Centralisation or Decentralisation: Alternative Strategies for Public Policy for Universities and Colleges in Canada 37
David M. Cameron

The Struggle for Higher Education Resources 49
Ralph G.M. Sultan and Paul E. Sultan

Policies for Access and Expansion in British Higher Education 69
John Barnes and Nicholas Barr

III. Governance and Accountability 87

The Governance and Funding of University Education in Britain: Retrospect and Prospect 89
Nigel F.B. Allington

Accountability and Autonomy in Canada's University Sector: Business as Usual or the Lull Before the Storm? 111
J. Cutt and Rod Dobell

IV. Open and Distance Education 135

The Open College of South London: A Development in Post-School Education 137
Margaret Bird

Distance Learning and Management Education: Developments and Prospects in the United Kingdom 151
Rob Paton

Post-Secondary Distance Education: Canada and the United Kingdom Compared 163
John S. Daniel

V. Private Sector Participation 173

An Example of Successful School/Industry Links: The East London Compact 175
J.F. Jarvis

Training and Development: The Shadow Higher
Education System in Canada 189
   Gilles Paquet

VI. Lloyds Bank Lecture 203

Education for Life and Work in the 1990s 205
   Sir Jeremy Morse

Annex A – Participants 213

Preface

These proceedings mark the fifth in a continuing series of colloquia on issues of current importance to Canada and the United Kingdom. The subject of the November 1988 Colloquium was post-secondary education with an emphasis on preparation for the world of work.

The transformations of the contemporary world which are intended to be captured in labels like 'the information society' or 'the new globalized economy' are changing dramatically the environment in which all education, perhaps especially post-secondary education, is carried on. Pressures for rapid adaptation of the labour force and constant adjustment of industrial structure place unprecedented demands on the ability of post-secondary institutions to indicate not only high levels of relevant skills but resilience, adaptability and acceptance of change in growing numbers of people engaged in continuing education in a variety of non-conventional settings, at all ages, as well as in traditional student bodies. Ultimately these pressures may persuade even faculty members clinging to the vestiges of a medieval environment that the twenty-first century is almost upon them.

Evident needs for more rapid innovation and diffusion of new technologies and procedure challenge the traditional institutions of research and research managements and force growing concerns for relevance and 'practicality'. Belated but growing recognition that human survival may well depend on fundamental change in our concepts of economic growth and in our modes of economic organization is plunging post-secondary institutions not only into controversy as to how the relevant scientific evidence should be developed and interpreted, but also into debate as to what role is appropriate in bringing about the necessary fundamental change in social attitudes and values and how social concepts of work should be altered in response.

Questions very much at the forefront of current controversy are the appropriate role of government in providing public services like education and training or in deploying powers of taxation to fund students or institutions; the appropriate role of business as partners in research undertakings or in initiatives to keep students in school; the effective processes to attack social problems which impede students' academic progress; and the effective methods to smooth the various transitions from school to work, from learning to labouring and back, with a continuing mix of formal learning and on other job training.

Similarly, increasing integration of computing and communication technologies leads to hard problems of balancing a public interest in broad access to information through assured openness and reduced barriers to information exchange against a public interest in a growing knowledge base achieved at least in part by more stringent concepts of intellectual property and tougher enforcement of barriers to information sharing. Again, what all this means for the way in which young people and older workers are to be helped to prepare for the new world of work is very puzzling.

All these issues are being faced in common by institutions in both Canada and the United Kingdom, from somewhat different starting points and against a background of somewhat different traditions and starting points. They are addressed in various ways in the papers which make up these proceedings of the 1988 Colloquium.

But the underlying premise is, of course, that we have a great deal to learn from each other through sharing the experience that has been gained in all our attempts to respond to the challenges of a world that is changing rapidly, inexorably, and in ways which increasingly seem to limit the autonomy and discretion even of nation states. The continued autonomy and discretion of post-secondary institutions in these circumstances seems likely to demand both greater responsiveness and vastly increased attention to accountability. The 1988 exchange of ideas and information seemed enormously interesting and stimulating to those participating; perhaps it can also be hoped that publication of these proceedings will also contribute to wider awareness of some of the ideas generated by that exchange.

In holding this Colloquium, the Institute for Research on Public Policy and the British Committee for the Canada-United Kingdom

Colloquia relied heavily on the valuable contributions of others. Lloyds Bank Canada provided a major portion of the funding to bring both Canadian and British participants to Mississauga, Ontario, Canada and we are happy to include in those proceedings the address given by Sir Jeremy Morse, Chairman of Lloyds Bank. Further support came from the Canadian Department of External Affairs and the British Foreign and Commonwealth Office.

I should like to express particular thanks to Professor Ronald Watts who served magnificently as Chairman of the Colloquium and subsequently as editor of these proceedings. He was admirably assisted in this latter capacity by Jeff Greenberg.

Like so many similar events, success depends on an effective infrastructure so that the participants can devote their time profitably to substantive discussions, without concern for the routine but essential arrangements which support them. The 1988 Colloquium was extremely well served in this respect by Denis Balsom, Peter Dobell and Lisa Peacock. For the compilation and editing of this book, we are indebted to Carol Seaborn, Debrah Kearns and Ruby Day.

This 1988 Colloquium was considered an unqualified success by the participants. We thank all the sponsors and participants for their contribution to this outcome.

Rod Dobell
President

Préface

Le présent ouvrage est un recueil des exposés présentés au cours du cinquième d'une série de colloques consacrés à des sujets d'actualité importants pour le Canada et le Royaume-Uni. Le colloque de novembre 1988 était consacré à l'enseignement postsecondaire et il était axé tout particulièrement sur la préparation au monde du travail.
 Les transformations que subit le monde contemporain et auxquelles on attribue des étiquettes comme 'société informatique' ou 'nouvelle économie globalisée', modifient radicalement le cadre dans lequel évoluent l'éducation en général, et surtout l'enseignement postsecondaire. La nécessité d'une adaptation rapide de la population active ainsi que d'un rajustement constant de la structure industrielle obligent plus que jamais les établissements postsecondaries non seulement à atteindre des niveaux de compétence élevés mais aussi à faire preuve d'une grande souplesse, d'une grande capacité d'adaptation et à accepter le fait qu'un nombre croissant de personnes s'adonnent à une certaine éducation permanente dans le cadre scolaire traditionnel et en dehors, à n'importe quel âge, ce qui finira peut-être par convaincre un jour les universitaires qui s'accrochent désespérément à un milieu médiéval que le XXIe siècle approche à pas de géant.
 Les établissements traditionnels de recherche et les responsables de la recherche sont appelés à faire face à la nécessité absolue d'innover et de diffuser plus rapidement les technologies nouvelles et à faire preuve de plus de réalisme et de sens pratique. On reconnaît, certes un peu

tard, mais de plus en plus, que la survie de l'humanité dépend peut-être d'une modification radicale de notre conception de la croissance économique et de nos modes d'organisation économique, ce qui plonge les établissements postsecondaires dans des polémiques sur la façon d'obtenir et d'interpréter des preuves scientifiques pertinentes et dans un débat sur le rôle qu'il convient de jouer pour changer complètement, comme il se doit, les attitudes et les valeurs sociales, et voir comment il convient de modifier en conséquence la notion du travail sur le plan social.

Les sujets qui reviennent le plus souvent dans les discussions à l'heure actuelle sont le rôle que doit jouer le gouvernement dans des services comme l'éducation et la formation ou le recours à ses pouvoirs fiscaux pour financer les étudiants et les établissements; le rôle des milieux d'affaires comme associés dans les recherches ou dans les initiatives visant à convaincre les étudiants de rester à l'école; les moyens efficaces de résoudre les problèmes sociaux que entravent les progrès scolaires des étudiants; et les méthodes efficaces pour amortir les différentes transitions de l'école au marché du travail, de l'apprentissage au marché du travail et vice versa en combinant continuellement la formation théorique et pratique.

Par ailleurs, en raison de l'intégration croissante des techniques d'informatique et de communication, il est très difficile d'arriver à concilier, dans l'intérêt public, le libre accès à l'information grâce à une ouverture garantie et à la suppression des obstacles entravant les échanges d'informations avec l'élargissement des connaissances grâce, en partie du moins, à une conception plus stricte de la propriété intellectuelle et une application plus stricte des règles de portage des informations. C'est un problème très intrigant car on se demande comment il faut s'y prendre pour aider les jeunes et les travailleurs d'un certain âge à se préparer au nouveau monde du travail.

Ces problèmes se posent à la fois au Canada et au Royaume-Uni, mais avec des origines et un cadre traditionnel légèrement différents. Ces problèmes sont abordés sous différents angles dans les exposés du colloque de 1988 qui forment le présent recueil.

Nous partons évidemment du principe que nous avons beaucoup à apprendre l'un de l'autre en partageant l'expérience acquise dans toutes les tentatives faites pour relever les défis d'un monde qui évolue rapidement, inexorablement, et qui prend des orientations susceptibles de limiter de plus en plus l'autonomie et la liberté d'action des États-nations. Pour permettre aux établissements postsecondaires de conserver leur autonomie dans ce climat, il faudra faire preuve d'une plus grande souplesse et d'un sens plus aigu des responsabilités. Les idées et les informations échangées au cours de ce colloque de 1988 sont apparemment très intéressantes et très stimulantes pour les participants; espérons que la publication du présent recueil contribuera également à véhiculer certaines des idées qui ont jailli de ces discussions.

Pour l'organisation du colloque, l'Institut de recherches politiques et le comité britannique des colloques Canada-Royaume-Uni ont compté largement sur l'aide financière extérieure. La Banque Lloyds du Canada a donné une bonne partie des fonds nécessaires pour réunir les participants canadiens et britanniques à Mississauga, en Ontario, Canada, et nous sommes heureux d'insérer dans ce recueil le discours prononcé par son président, Sir Jeremy Morse. Nous avons également reçu de l'aide du ministère des Affaires extérieures du Canada et du ministère des affaires étrangères du Royaume-Uni.

Je tiens à remercier tout particulièrement le professeur Ronald Watts, qui a joué à merveille son rôle de président du colloque et qui a eu l'obligeance de vérifier le présent recueil, tâche dans laquelle il a été admirablement secondé par Jeff Greenberg.

Comme pour bien d'autres manifestations analogues, la réussite dépend d'une organisation efficace permettant aux participants de se consacrer entièrement à des discussions de fond sans devoir se soucier des services de soutien habituels mais essentiels. A cet égard, nous devons beaucoup à Denis Balsom, à Peter Dobell et à Lisa Peacock. Nous remercions également Carol Seaborn, Debrah Kearns et Ruby Day pour la compilation et la vérification du présent recueil.

Le colloque de 1988 est considéré comme une réussite totale par les participants. Nous remercions tous les commanditaires et tous les participants.

Rod Dobell
Président

Introduction
RONALD L. WATTS, QUEEN'S UNIVERSITY, CANADA

Both the United Kingdom and Canada are currently grappling with the need to reassess their public policies for post-secondary education in the face of new realities. Two major factors have contributed to this rethinking about the role of post-secondary education within society. First, there has been the emergence of the information society changing the context within which universities and colleges are having to operate. Under the impact of the post-industrial revolution since the 1970s the radical transformation from an industrial society to a knowledge-based one has produced a new emphasis upon the importance of post-secondary education and research for the development of society. Closely related to this has been the growing global economic interdependence. This has led to a recognition that post-secondary education and research are important instruments contributing to a nation's international economic competitiveness and to prosperity. From this perspective, the cost of supporting education in universities and colleges is not so much a problem as an essential part of the solution. Consequently, post-secondary education is seen as an investment in the development of valuable human capital, and academic research and scholarship as an investment in the development of knowledge essential to the adaptiveness, growth and vigour of society.

A second and equally important factor focussing attention upon post-secondary education has been the increasing emphasis upon education as a means to increasing social equity and mobility. Growing attention has fastened upon post-secondary education not only in terms of how it can contribute to national economic, social and cultural development, but also in terms of how it can provide the means for greater social equity, social mobility, and equality of opportunity.

At this time when changes in society are forcing a rethinking of the role of post-secondary education in both the United Kingdom and Canada, similar fundamental questions about the appropriate focus of post-secondary education are being raised in both countries. First, what should be the main functions and objectives of universities and colleges faced with the challenge of these radical changes in society? Are there conflicts between these functions and can priorities be specified? Closely related is the question of how the functions of the different institutions of post-secondary education, the universities and colleges, relate to each other? Second, is the contribution which universities and colleges can make to society enhanced by public policies and funding arrangements focussed on reinforcing the co-ordinated direction of these institutions, or by policies that emphasize decentralization and institutional variety and initiative? Third, given the clear value and importance of post-secondary education to national development and social equity, how can greater efficiency, effectiveness and public accountability in the performance of these institutions be ensured without undermining their vitality and innovative spirit? Fourth, can new and imaginative forms of open and distance education improve the development of the nation's human resources and the equality of opportunity for citizens? Fifth, what are the emerging trends in the role of the private sector in post-secondary education both in terms of greater co-operation with existing universities and colleges and in terms of the provision of alternative corporate programmes to fulfil needs not being met by the universities and colleges?

It was to address these issues that the Canada-United Kingdom Colloquium on 'Post-Secondary Education: Preparation for the World of Work', was held in Mississauga, Ontario, Canada, November 20-22, 1988. This volume contains revised versions of the papers presented on that occasion. A full list of the British and Canadian participants is given in the appendix to this volume and the programme of the colloquium is included there.

The discussions in the colloquium in Mississauga proved highly interesting. Participants from both countries agreed at the end that the calibre and intensity of discussion had been extremely high and that each group had learned a great deal from the other. The gathering was particularly useful not only in identifying common concerns, but also in making participants aware of otherwise unrecognized differences between the two countries. Thus the colloquium provided a process contributing to mutual understanding that was felt to be of benefit to both. Moreover, given the current degree of ferment in the world of higher education, the comparative analysis contributed new insights for each group into the issues and into appropriate policies for their own countries.

Not surprisingly, on most issues attention was drawn not only to points of similarity but also to differences between the two countries. Four points of difference drew particular attention. The first arose in the discussion of the interrelationship between quality and participation within post-secondary education. While a major British concern seemed to be how an essentially elite system of post-secondary education might obtain the resources to broaden participation in it, the Canadian concern focussed primarily on how, having achieved a broad participation in post-secondary education, resources might be ensured to enhance and maintain quality. Two simple statistics illustrate the different bases from which the participants from the two countries approached this balance. Where for every 100,000 of population Canada annually produces 616 higher education graduates annually, the comparable British figure is 280.[1] But in terms of expenditure per student Canada spends only 66 per cent of that spent by the United Kingdom.[2] This contrast, of course, must not be overdrawn. There are concerns in Britain about ensuring the quality of post-secondary education, and there are continuing concerns in Canada about areas where, in the interests of social justice, expansion of participation in post-secondary education needs to be further encouraged. Among notable examples are the First Canadians (Canada's native peoples), women in certain professional programmes, francophones outside Quebec, and those living in the remoter areas. Nevertheless, the contrast between the two countries in their main concerns was clear.

A second important point of difference between the two countries which affected the discussion of many of the issues was the contrast between their frameworks for public policy making. Britain's unitary constitutional structure gives to Westminster an ability to make or even impose radical national changes in policy relating to post-secondary education which Canada's federal system, with its divided and shared jurisdiction between federal and provincial governments, constrains. The Canadian constitution assigns jurisdiction over education to the provinces, but many areas which clearly fall within the federal domain or shared federal-provincial responsibility, such as those relating to the development of the economy and the encouragement of research, are closely related to the basic activities of contemporary universities and colleges. Thus, there has developed a long history in Canada of a shared interest on the part of both the federal and provincial governments in the support of universities and colleges and of research. It is not only the requirement of joint federal-provincial action which constrains the development of coherent national policies relating to post-secondary education in Canada. The political strength of regionalism and the emphasis upon different priorities and interests in various provinces has made reaching agreement upon coherent national policies particularly difficult. The other side to this contrast with Britain, however, is that the Canadian federal system has allowed some provinces to experiment with innovations without having to wait for nation-wide agreement upon a uniform national policy.

A third significant difference between the two countries affecting policy relating to post-secondary education is the contrasting size and distribution of their populations. The population of the United Kingdom is both much larger and geographically more compact than Canada's smaller and continentally dispersed population. This has led to different emphases, for example, in the form and character of open learning and distance education programmes in the two countries.

Finally, while post-secondary education in both countries is marked by a combination of universities and colleges, the role of polytechnics in Britain and the resulting binary character of the degree granting institutions there has, with only a few exceptions, no real parallel in Canada. Where the word 'university' is more or less synonymous in Canada with 'degree giving institution', polytechnics in Britain represent a major group of degree granting institutions, educating something like 50 per cent of the full-time students in higher education and offering the main route for continuing and vocational education. In Canada, on the other hand, of a total full-time enrolment in post-secondary education of 1.1 million, 71 per cent are enrolled in universities and the other 29 per cent are enrolled in the diploma programmes of the colleges which generally do not offer degrees. This contrast has important implications for the different roles played by universities and colleges in relation to each other within each of the two countries.

But while there are significant differences in the context and structure within which post-secondary education is provided in the two countries, the colloquium had no difficulty in identifying a number of areas of common concern where the sharing of views proved helpful. The first of these related to the challenges facing our systems of post-secondary education. There was general agreement on the urgency of responding effectively to the challenge posed by the increasingly knowledge-based character of society and the competitive global economy, a thrust which Geraldine Kenney-Wallace's opening contribution emphasized. John Rae examined, from a British perspective, the relationship between education and economic growth. This led a number of participants to suggest that, although a substantial international literature has developed in this relationship, we still need to pin down the precise linkages between education and economic growth. There was also considerable interest on the part of participants in the significance of the epistemology of learning as exemplified by the impact of a vocational focus on learning and motivation. At the same time emphasis was put on the importance of education directed not at pigeon-holing for a specific vocation, but at providing a base for a life-time of personal development. A point that was echoed by a number of contributors, particularly Geraldine Kenney-Wallace, Rod Dobell and Gilles Paquet, was that in responding to the challenges facing society in both countries, universities and colleges, as agents of change in society, need to be ready to change themselves. A further point that attracted discussion was the balance between education geared to enhancing economic efficiency and social justice. While these could be in conflict, a number of participants argued that this need not be the case and that as dual objectives they should complement each other.

The sessions of the colloquium on co-ordination versus decentralization and on governance and accountability also identified common concerns among the participants from both countries relating to the way in which the provision of post-secondary education should be organized. David Cameron converted the issue of centralization versus decentralization into an analysis of the relative merits and dangers of governmental co-ordination versus institutional competition within systems of post-secondary education. John Barnes and Nicholas Barr addressed the issue by proposing for Britain a system in which higher education institutions would be left to conduct their affairs as they wish. This would be achieved through a system of government funding students rather than institutions. Thus, students would be assisted by loans whose repayment would be related to their subsequent earnings. Interestingly, Ralph Sultan advocated a somewhat similar solution for Canada. Nigel Allington, after reviewing the history of developments in Britain, concluded that academic excellence and academic freedom had proved incompatible with state control of universities and urged a policy of gradual privatisation of post-secondary education. Rod Dobell, in addressing accountability and autonomy in Canada's university sector took a quite different tack. He noted how elsewhere, particularly in Britain, governments were demanding greater accountability on the part of universities in meeting national needs. He went on to raise the question whether, given the scale of public funds being provided, Canadian universities are showing enough initiative and imagination in responding to public concerns about their performance. This led to considerable discussion of the issues of tenure and unionization as constraints upon responsiveness to change in the two countries.

The third area of common interest related to new modes for provision for post-secondary education as represented by open learning and distance education programmes and by private sector participation. In the area of open learning and distance education Margaret Bird, Rob Paton and John Daniel outlined a variety of innovative arrangements that have been developed in Britain and Canada. As John Daniel pointed out, there are some significant differences between the two countries due to differing historical and demographic circumstances. But there was general agreement that interaction between the British and Canadian traditions would be fruitful in terms of what each could learn from the other. In addition, the contribution of technological advances to open and distance learning was noted, but it was also recognized that there was a danger in being mesmerized by technology: often low technology works best in reaching out to the public. The importance of marketing and of relating policies and expectations to each other was also emphasized. The need for open learning and distance education programmes to take account of the requirement for adult education and interdisciplinary studies directed at longer-term personal adaptability was also stressed.

Participation of the private sector in post-secondary education was reviewed from two quite different perspectives. Freddie Jarvis outlined some very interesting examples of school-industry links and this led to a review of the variety of co-operative arrangements between the private sector and the institutions of post-secondary education in each of the two countries. Gilles Paquet on the other hand drew attention to the rapid growth in recent years in North America of a whole range of post-secondary education programmes provided by the private sector as alternatives to those provided by the traditional post-secondary education institutions. He raised the question of whether this had been the result of a lack of responsiveness to social needs on the part of the traditional institutions.

Inevitably, in the two days of discussion, the colloquium was not able to deal as fully as it might have liked with each subject. The discussion concentrated rather too much perhaps on the university as the primary post-secondary education vehicle at the expense of proper attention to other institutions of post-secondary learning. A fuller discussion of the relative roles and relationship to each other of universities and colleges would have been desirable. There could, as well have been more discussion on the role of teachers and on the relationship of education and research to each other (and of the methods of funding them). At the end there was also some discussion as to whether the colloquium had adequately clarified the nature of the world of work for which post-secondary education was preparing people. It was appropriate, therefore, that Sir Jeremy Morse, in his closing address to the colloquium, concentrated his remarks on this subject.

If complacency is the greatest danger to an effective response on the part of post-secondary education in the United Kingdom and Canada to the challenge of change, there was little complacency apparent in the discussions at the colloquium. The discussions pointed to exciting developments and imaginative ideas in variety of areas in both countries. For all the problems that beset post-secondary education in our two countries, the colloquium provided encouraging signs that there are real prospects for future development.

Notes

1. Commonwealth Tertiary Education Commission, *Review of efficiency and effectiveness in higher education* (Canberra: Australian Government Publishing Service, 1986), p. 104. Comparable figures for other countries are: U.S.A. 621, Japan 432, Australia 430, West Germany 270.

2. Report of the Universities Review Committee to the New Zealand Vice Chancellors' Committee, *New Zealand's Universities: Partners in National Development* (Washington, N.Z.: New Zealand Vice Chancellors' Committee, 1987), p. 20.

I
THE CHALLENGE OF CHANGE

The Challenge of Change for 2001: The Canadian University in a Knowledge-Intensive Society

DR. GERALDINE A. KENNY-WALLACE
CHAIRMAN, SCIENCE COUNCIL OF CANADA

Science and society are so tightly interwoven in the fabric of the modern industrialized world that it is almost impossible to unravel the two. And yet they have always been so intertwined. It is what we perceive as science that changes in time, and our personal perspectives evolve in a slowly changing society. Science of yesterday, such as solid state physics, becomes encapsulated in a modern convenience of today, such as a microwave oven. However, the appreciation of science and modern standards of scientific literacy do not match this transition.

The university, through scholarship in research and teaching and the dissemination and advancement of knowledge, is one of the key threads in this fabric. And it is becoming an increasingly important one as society becomes more and more knowledge-intensive. Contemporary pressures are pulling the fabric out of its familiar shape. The unease is global in its dimensions. From Europe to North America, from Asia to U.S.S.R., I hear tales of passion for academic freedom mixed with personal frustration bouncing off the wall of criticism from the private sector and from society at large that universities have lost their sense of direction. Of course, the reality is somewhere in between. What everyone agrees upon, is that the roles of the university and the scholar and student are under severe questioning both from the inside and the outside. Instinctively, when we want to learn about the latest, bright idea we usually seek out individuals in universities. Yet, curiously, universities are also some of the most conservative institutions in society today. To quote Dr. Ron Watts, the chairman of our meeting:

> Paradoxically, universities, the most traditional of institutions, are now faced with the challenge of adapting rapidly enough to survive the conditions that they themselves, through the advancement of knowledge, have created.

While some might argue that Dr. Watts has given universities too much credit for our changing circumstances, I agree with him that evolution and adaptation to the needs of a knowledge-intensive society is the challenge. It is a challenge for change, and a challenge to seek commitment to change from the scholarly community. In fact, we are really addressing the wise management of change for the twenty-first century as the fabric of society is rewoven into new global patterns based upon strategic alliances, whose origins lie in the dramatically shifting trade relationships among countries and the reality of 'offshore' manufacturing.

While scholars will always debate and argue positions, often with eloquence, the challenge for change facing all industrialized societies is one of international competitiveness. The challenge is unequivocally linked to economic renewal and survival as a civilized society, as we position ourselves in the wake of a new economic paradigm for 2001. The challenge, sometimes admitted and sometimes ignored, is necessarily driving the university role into sharp focus. In Canada, the focus is on the university research—innovation interface. The call to intellectual arms for economic revitalization demands a higher flux of activity at that innovation interface in order to create a more substantive indigenous R&D base within our industrial base. Whether cooperative R&D projects, educational linkages, student and faculty exchange, or university-industry research institutes, the linkages must be dynamic and tailored to each situation. What is common to all is the imperative that such linkages are essential to Canadian competitiveness in this unusual period of transition. What are the policy issues involved and what are the R&D priorities?

Unfortunately, in a subject such as this one, it is all too easy to lose the forest for the trees. For example, earlier this year, a meeting of policy researchers on higher education from Canadian governments and educational associations resulted in a list of 54 priority research and policy issues. We also tend to confuse challenges and responses, although it is true they are related. Last year, the National Forum on Post-Secondary Education sponsored by the Secretary of State and by the Council of Ministers of Education, Canada, raised a number of these challenges and responses that were on the minds of many

Canadians. Among them were accessibility; excellence; balance between research and teaching; the desirable differences between the mandates of the plethora of institutions ensuring quality education; the need for broader participation in higher education especially among Canada's first nations, the disabled, immigrants, mature students, women students; the development of better links between the research and teaching levels of higher education; the need for more student aid; and the concern for greater accountability. Several of these topics are on the agenda of this meeting.

While all of these topics are important, they strike me more as responses to external challenges. All too often the focus of discussion about the crisis facing our universities is on the infrastructure or the quality of students as the input to the university system, or on the internal complex workings of that system. The challenge of change means that we have to focus on outputs of the system, on the quality of the graduates, on university goals and their achievement. I also sometimes feel that many of the former topics fall into the category of old responses to new challenges. More of the same, even if we were to agree on what comprised 'the same', is not the answer to the present crisis of underfunding and (possibly unfairly) public perceptions. This may well be the time to face structural change for the whole system.

Canadian universities will be hard pressed to meet the challenge of change given their present capacity to respond after decades of deficits. On the one hand, money is a critical factor in the ability of universities to respond adequately to society's expectations. There is no doubt that the stresses on our universities have been compounded in turn by financial restraint compounded again by rising costs and increasing demands. Table 1 shows that in Canada, as in many other countries, enrolments have grown faster than public expenditures on higher education.

But a consensus also appears to be emerging that despite the clear evidence of financial need, solving the problems facing Canadian universities requires more imagination and wise management of all resources than simply more money. In Table 2, statistics show that Canadians are already spending a higher percentage of gross domestic product on higher education than most other countries.

On the other hand, Canadian universities face mounting external criticism. Our universities, in the opinion of many Canadians, are not wholly suited to the current and emerging challenges of the country. If more money is to be directed to universities, universities and those who fund them should address first a deeper problem of the institution, 'a more generalized malaise of purpose.'

Table 1
Growth of Enrolments and Real Public Expenditure on Higher Education between 1970 and 1983

Country	Expenditure[a]	Enrolment
Austria	49.4%	157.8%
Canada	3.9	62.2
Denmark	-7.0	45.7
Finland	104.4	100.7
France	-25.0	47.2
Germany	29.9	179.0
Italy	24.2	49.8
Japan	27.6	31.5
Luxembourg	46.8	159.9
Netherlands	21.6	64.6
New Zealand	-7.7	35.0
Norway	43.0	64.9
Sweden	-29.9	53.2
United Kingdom	-4.8	42.8
United States	13.6	46.2

Note:
a. Adjusted using OECD educational expenditure deflators.

Source: Organization for Economic Cooperation and Development. *Costs, expenditures and Financing: An Analysis of Trends*, ED(86)10, 1986, 163.

Our universities are in a difficult position. They have to cope with dwindling resources as governments attempt to control public spending. At the same time they have to cope with demands for greater accountability as interest groups outside the university try to inject their own agenda. The result is a paradox: universities appear to be in decline at the same time as the public is attaching a growing importance to them and challenging them to change. These unsettling times can feel threatening to some. Under leadership, these times are an opportunity to shift intellectual and management gears and position a vital resource of scholarship, knowledge and research for the 21st century.

Table 2
Public Expenditure on Higher Education as a Percentage of Gross Domestic Product (GDP)

Country	Percentage of GDP
Australia	1.58
Austria	0.77
Canada	2.00
Finland	0.89
France	0.69[a]
Germany	0.59
Italy	0.53
Japan	0.41[a]
Netherlands	1.76[a]
New Zealand	0.11
Norway	0.79
Sweden	0.62
United Kingdom	1.09[a]
United States	2.49[b]

Notes:
a. Data from 1982.
b. Data from 1981.

Source: Based on UNESCO *Statistical Yearbook 1986*, Paris, Table 4.3.

Fortunately, we in Canada have reason for optimism. In the past, our universities have demonstrated an ability to evolve with society. For example, at the turn of the century, largely in response to demands from a more industrialized economy, they began to raise the profile of research to the same level as that of undergraduate education as an essential function of a university. Today, universities are faced with the demand for a similar kind of evolution, and they seem to be recognizing this challenge for strategic partnerships with other sectors of society. Last month's *University Affairs*, a newspaper put out by the Association of Universities and Colleges of Canada, contained a special report entitled 'Time for new blueprint'. Its message was that 'the time has come for universities to re-think their goals and priorities. Universities must rearticulate where they stand—and what they stand for in society.' A constructive period of renewal is necessary in any long-standing institution after two generations. After 800 years, the university as an institution can renew itself without fear!

Now, I would claim that the key to understanding the nature of the overall economic and intellectual challenge to our universities and how they can respond lies in an examination of the emerging knowledge-intensive society. It is the demand for specialists and research-driven programmes that are in apparent conflict with the older thrusts of liberal education and teaching priorities. It is not impossible to do both well. It is unforgivable to do both badly. As a case study therefore, I want to concentrate on the economic challenge facing Canada and its implications for our own universities. There are analogies to other countries. I would further claim that in the response of our universities to this challenge we can see the direction in which all of our universities will have to evolve, to adapt and to lead society as a whole.

Canada now confronts a world economy of tradeable goods and services that is moving to a new level of R&D knowledge-intensiveness. The global market for low technology goods is becoming saturated but demands for services and high technology goods is growing. In such conditions, science-based innovation and technological innovation in both service industries and goods-producing industries are more than ever the key to improving economic performance. They are the engine of economic growth. To maintain competitiveness, Canada must use new technologies to revitalize mature industries and generate new high-technology industries. More science and technology, more R&D and superior management of technology become the raw material of this engine. Our graduates must not only be literate in a scientific and technological sense but be educated rigorously in the 'great books' and appreciative of the labour and financial markets as well.

Canada's economy is changing, but there are indications that it is still not doing so rapidly enough. Although 'high tech' goods are becoming an increasingly important segment of international trade and Canada is both importing and exporting more such goods, our balance of trade deficit in this area is growing. Our industrial technology appears to be relatively underdeveloped compared to that of other advanced countries. Indeed, the graphs in Figure 1 need different vertical scales to display changes in national trade balances. Furthermore, the ability of Canadian businesses to adopt and adapt new ideas and processes quickly and effectively leaves much to be desired (Figure 2). Canada gets poor ratings for innovation.

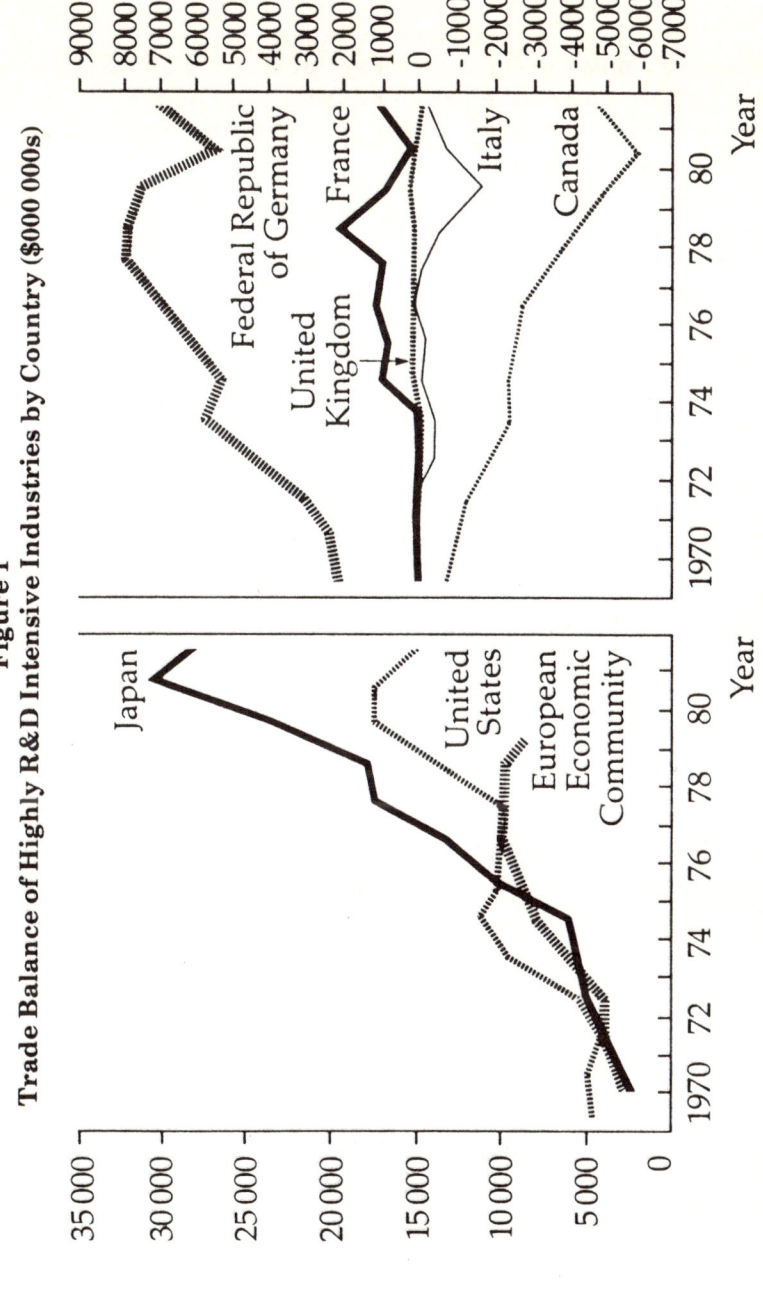

Figure 1
Trade Balance of Highly R&D Intensive Industries by Country ($000 000s)

Source: Ministry of State for Science and Technology, *Science, Technology and Economic Development: A Working Paper* (Ottawa, 1985), 38.

**Figure 2
Forward Orientation.**
This indicator measures the commercial sector's ability in long-range planning and flexibility in adapting to change. It covers criteria related to the development of technology and its role in fostering competitiveness.

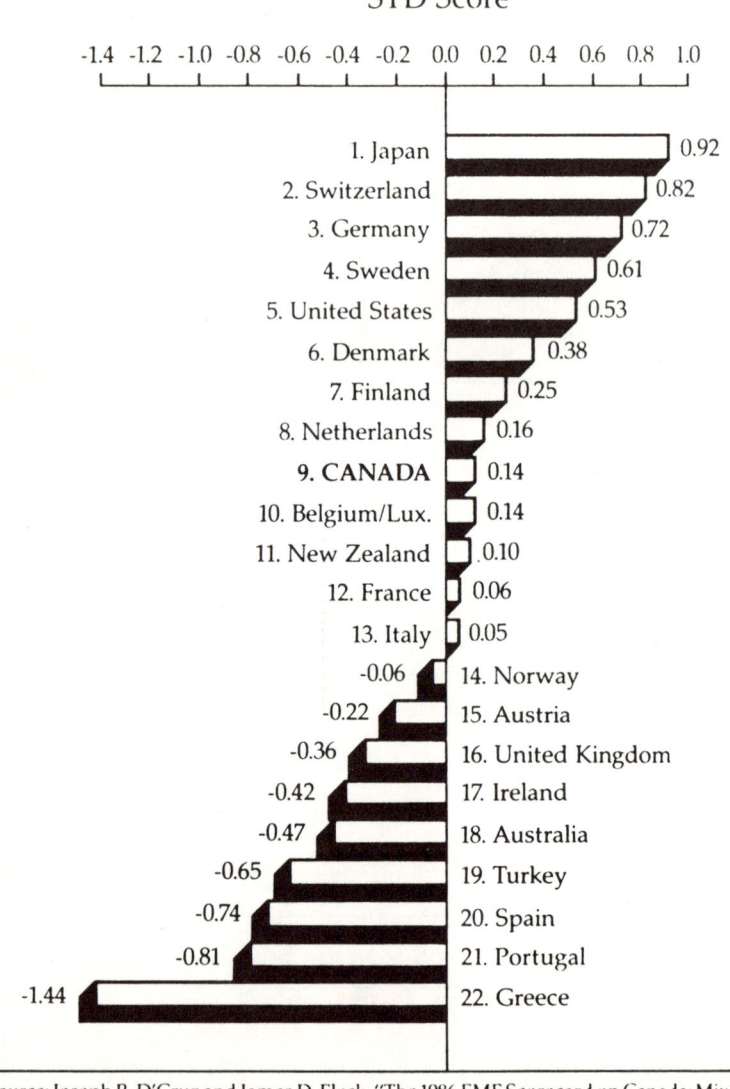

Rank	Country	STD Score
1.	Japan	0.92
2.	Switzerland	0.82
3.	Germany	0.72
4.	Sweden	0.61
5.	United States	0.53
6.	Denmark	0.38
7.	Finland	0.25
8.	Netherlands	0.16
9.	**CANADA**	0.14
10.	Belgium/Lux.	0.14
11.	New Zealand	0.10
12.	France	0.06
13.	Italy	0.05
14.	Norway	-0.06
15.	Austria	-0.22
16.	United Kingdom	-0.36
17.	Ireland	-0.42
18.	Australia	-0.47
19.	Turkey	-0.65
20.	Spain	-0.74
21.	Portugal	-0.81
22.	Greece	-1.44

Source: Joseph R. D'Cruz and James D. Fleck, "The 1986 EMF Scorecard on Canada: Mixed but Encouraging," *Business Quarterly* 51:2 (Summer 1986), 85.
*The STD Score measures the competitiveness of a country compared with all the other 21 OECD countries in the study.

In response to the challenge of economic renewal, our universities are going to have to play a more direct role in maintaining the international competitiveness of the Canadian economy. They are, of course, only one part of the solution to our economic problems. Other educational sectors, all levels of government, and industry, especially, have roles to play. In fact, in gearing up for a global economy, it is indeed the private sector's challenge and commitment to create and sustain an indigenous R&D base and an ethos of innovation in order to ensure longer-term prosperity. Consensus is required to determine exactly how. Universities, however, are a necessary factor in economic renewal. If Canada is to prosper and the university is to flourish, the *status quo* is not an option. Economic renewal and intellectual renewal are inextricably linked. In part this is because the historical facts have led to an industrial mix in Canada that reflects our once prosperous resource-based economy and the private sector does not find itself fully capable of dealing with the market challenges of a technology-intensive area. The research-innovation interface thus becomes a critical function across which ideas and people must flow. We can no longer rely on the natural comparative advantage of fish and forests, minerals, oil and grains. We must create our own comparative advantage, through value-added R&D and science-based innovation targeted to these strengths, and through research, innovation and invention.

From evidence around the industrialized world the university's role in the economy is already changing. Canada is no exception. University-industry interaction is in a state of ferment in Canada. Within the last decade, Canadian universities have taken a large number of initiatives aimed at developing closer links with industry. The Science Council of Canada, in a recent study of these initiatives, was encouraged to discover that much more experimentation is going on than is widely recognised. We identified at least three major ways in which universities usefully foster collaboration with industry-university services to support linkages such as innovation centres, R&D linkages, and educational linkages. Whatever mechanisms are explored for the diffusion and promotion of ideas and people, quality must be the overriding criterion.

Let me develop a little further just one of these three categories—that of educational linkages. Increased university-business collaboration in this area presents three challenges, or three opportunities for universities. The first is a challenge to broaden the scope of the curriculum. One of the responses by universities that we in the Council found, consisted of a rapid growth in courses on the management of technological innovation and technical entrepreneurship. The second challenge is better integration of formal learning and of 'real world' experience. A response to this challenge that we found across Canada is cooperative education, a variant on 'sandwich course' programmes in the United Kingdom. The third challenge to universities is to broaden their clientele beyond the traditional group of young and full-time students, and to fulfil their educational function in new and important ways. A response here is the development of tailored courses or seminars to address the continuing education needs of firms. Indeed, in Canada, the notion of life-long learning seems to have caught on surprisingly well.

This much progress has been made in linking universities and industry. A new, positive attitude has emerged about the role universities can play in the economy. Yet the future of these fledgling linkages, of these responses to the economic challenge, is by no means assured. Most have not taken full root in the university. And the level of interaction is far from what is needed and from what universities are capable of, given the intensity of the economic threats and rising deficits we face. The demand-side from industry is still too short term for the strategic partnerships to flourish without disruptive tensions.

There are two basic deterrents that will need to be overcome if the university is to respond fully to a knowledge-intensive economy. The first and primary deterrent is the widely held image of the university as an ivory tower—as an institution set apart from society. A new image of the university is required, one that fosters meeting the needs of a knowledge-intensive economy and society. Some say a platinum value-added tower is on the horizon!

Overcoming Deterrents

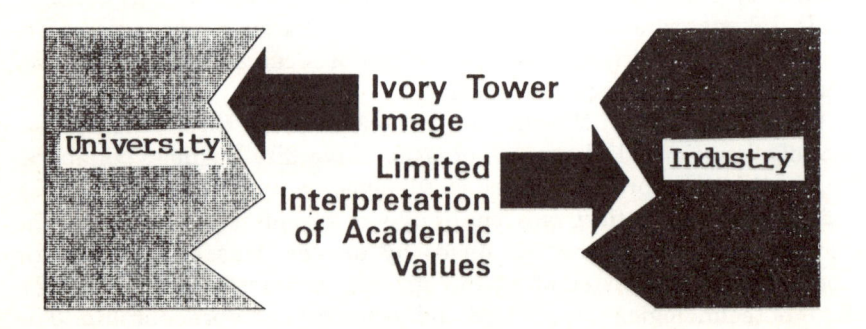

Science Council of Canada / Conseil des sciences du Canada

University ← Ivory Tower Image / Limited Interpretation of Academic Values → Industry

The second major deterrent comes from concerns about academic values. There is some apprehension that university-industry interaction threatens academic freedom, the free exchange of ideas, the pursuit of knowledge for its own sake and teaching and research as academic priorities. But academic values can be furthered, not necessarily subverted, through university-industry interaction. Linkages can be the means for the university to disseminate its values as well as to improve the placement of its graduates and to enhance the utility of its research. A focus on excellence and quality at all times will ensure respect and private sector support.

Science Council of Canada   Conseil des sciences du Canada

The University in a Knowledge-Intensive Economy

Traditional Role
- Liberal Education
- Fundamental Research

New Responsibilities
- Industry Collaboration
- Knowledge and Technology Transfer
- Targetted Research
- Education for a Technological Society

A reassessment of the university's mission is necessary to resolve the crisis in Canadian universities, to meet its great challenge. Universities cannot and must not abandon their traditional concerns with liberal education and fundamental research. The detraction of liberal education, however, must be broad enough to reflect the reality of the future and the need for more appreciation of inter-disciplinary and lateral thinking. At the same time, universities must accept the expanded role they are being called on to play in today's knowledge-intensive economy. Universities must improve their collaboration with industry in both research and education. They must reorient some of their activities to provide education for today's workers and targeted research for the private and public sectors. And the rewards system must recognize that those activities are a legitimate part of what universities do and that they are an essential function of the universities we will need.

I have given you a glimpse of how Canadian universities are beginning to respond to the challenge of economic renewal facing our country, and of what they must do if they are to meet the challenge fully. It only remains for me to remind you that this university-industry interaction is but a microcosm of the university-society interaction we will need in the future. In the 'new' university that is needed for Canada's emerging knowledge-intensive society, the present ways of teaching and performing research would not be displaced so much as reoriented. The essence of this university would be rigorous, critical and thoughtful enquiry in a dynamic, integral relationship with society. This indeed is the essence of scholarship that transcends the centuries and the borders of both discipline and geography.

In recognizing the transfer of knowledge and technology to society and industry as an integral and valued university activity, the university must ensure a balance and mutual reinforcement among its functions. Teaching and research should not be totally oriented toward meeting social needs or the present-day needs of the economy. A balance is necessary between those needs on the one side and, on the other, the value of a liberal education and of advancement of knowledge for its own sake. Otherwise the singular mandate of the student and scholar to push forward those frontiers of his or her imagination will be unfulfilled and the best and bright minds of any generation will choose institutions other than universities and colleges to meet their intellectual challenges. Neither can any university be expected to address all of the problems of society or the opportunities presented to it. The institution and its faculty have to set priorities. Furthermore, the requirement to transfer knowledge and technology for wealth-creation or for the good of society does not apply merely to the university's science and engineering departments. Society in a knowledge-intensive economy has a great need for the knowledge available in the humanities and social sciences. All parts of the university must explore how they can fulfil the institution's mission. There are indeed desirable differences between institutions, between faculties, between professors. There is a greater danger in confusing too many roles. Too much focus on accessibility alone without regard for mission, quality of graduates and an understanding of the particular role of the institution within the full spectrum of educational activity can lead to an unwieldy, over-expensive and poor quality result.

Some risks are involved in giving greater importance to the outreach or service function of the university. But the greatest danger to the Canadian university is that it will not search for ways to fulfil its mission that are suited to the needs of the knowledge-intensive economy and society. Universities must continue to evolve and play a more active role in Canadian society and the economy. If they do not change, their role will diminish as alternative ways are found of obtaining the teaching and research that are required by those outside the university milieu. Involvement in society and collaboration with industry, far from being a distraction, are a necessary part of the university's destiny. Intellectually, stimulation comes from inside one's mind, and these evolutionary and revolutionary notions can serve only to revitalize the university and its proud history of scholarship and scholars.

Education, Economic Prosperity and the Role of the State: Britain's Problem in Perspective

JOHN RAE
DIRECTOR, LAURA ASHLEY FOUNDATION

Once you link education with preparation for the world of work and set out to consider—as this session does—ways for educational institutions to be more responsive to the training needs of the economy you enter upon a fundamental debate about the nature and purpose of education. The British do not like fundamental debates about the nature and purpose of anything: to discuss the aims of education seems to them rather pretentious like discussing the meaning of life. This dislike of first principles has many advantages but in the case of educational reform it can persuade the British that tinkering with the system is the same as changing it.

I want to consider two fundamental questions that underlie this Colloquium and relate them to Britain's Education Reform Act of 1988, the most important piece of legislation affecting schools and universities since the state started to take responsibility for education in 1890. The two fundamental questions I have in mind are:

1. How far should education be geared to the needs of the state?

2. What is the connection between education and economic prosperity?

Education and the Needs of the State

If I may play the schoolmaster, I wonder if you can place in time and nationality these two statements:

> 'I too am a father; but my son does not belong to me. He belongs to the Republic. It is for her to decide what he ought to do in order to serve her well.'

> 'Education is not for the sake of the student but for the sake of the state.'

The point of asking is that we would all know at once that these statements could not have been made by an Englishman. That is not our way of doing things. Children are not the property of the state nor is education primarily for the sake of the state. We believe that such an attitude is incompatible with freedom and democracy, unless it is 'totalitarian democracy' and incompatible too with the tradition of liberal education that we have inherited from the Renaissance.

The authors of these statements must therefore belong to some form of totalitarian democracy or to some country that had the misfortune to miss out on the Renaissance. And we would be right. The first is Georges Danton addressing the French Revolutionary Convention in 1793 and the second is Arinori Mori, the Japanese minister of education 1885-1889.

Fifty years ago, Twenty years ago, we would have felt thankful that such sentiments were totally alien to Britain, that our education system was not harnessed to the chariot of the state. Central control and direction of education was anathema, a characteristic of less fortunate lands associated with a long line of continental bogeymen from Napoleon to Hitler. Only 11 years ago, in 1977, the education spokesmen of the two major political parties, Shirley Williams and Norman St. John Stevas, 'both rejected the idea of a common core curriculum imposed on schools by central government'.

In 1988, Britain at last got around to doing what Danton and Arinori Mori would have approved and imposed a National Curriculum. Was the British laissez faire attitude to education a virtue or a weakness? Did it represent a triumph of freedom and the Renaissance ideal or just an accident of geography?

I do not think it was a virtue. British education remained free for so long from state interference because the state had no interest in interfering. Britain was not seriously threatened with invasion: the state did not need to harness education to the military need for engineers, artillery officers and so on. Britain's economic power and imperial markets did not prompt politicians to ask until late in the

19th century whether there might be a connection between education and economic competitiveness. Even then hostility to the idea of strong central government meant that while a system of elementary education was established, the minister responsible had virtually no power to influence what was taught. That remained the position for over a 100 years, until this year 1988.

This British attitude to education, that is that it was not the concern of the government, encouraged and reflected the so-called liberal tradition. Until very recently every independent school prospectus assured parents that their children would receive a 'liberal education' at a moderate cost. Now that 'liberal' has become a term of abuse in Britain, the prospectuses have changes. Nowadays, Britain's independent schools, no less than the advocates of the new City Technology Colleges, stress the utilitarian nature of the education they offer. They reflect the changing climate in Britain's education system. What exactly is—or perhaps I should say was—the liberal ideal in education? The 15th century Italian humanist Vittorino de Feltre gives the classic definition: 'We call those studies "liberal" which are worthy of a free man'. Liberal education meant encouraging the student to think for himself, to develop discrimination, a critical faculty; it meant the study of pure subjects rather than applied, physics rather than technology; and it meant education that was free from the direction and control of the state.

The liberal tradition was in marked contrast to the approach in countries where education was seen from the start as the servant of the state. The circumstances varied but all these countries had a history of strong central government. Whether it was Peter the Great establishing schools to produce the civil servants and technical experts that Russia needed in the early 18th century; or the French Committee of Public Safety creating the Ecole Polytechnique in 1794 to produce the military and civil engineers to fight the revolutionary wars; or the Japanese gearing their education system to the task of catching up with the west in the late 19th century—the underlying assumption was always the same: education exists primarily for the sake of the state.

The choice that all countries have to make is not of course between completely laissez faire education on one hand and education totally subordinated to the needs of the state on the other. Countries choose their place on the spectrum according not only to their perceived needs but also to their culture and their political tradition. We can see the spectrum today: state control of education is tighter in France than in the United States, tighter in Japan than in France, tighter in the Soviet Union than in Japan, and so on. What has been happening in Britain in recent years is that the state has been moving slowly and reluctantly along the spectrum from laissez faire towards greater state control. The Education Reform Act this year, or more precisely that section that imposes a National Curriculum, is the first decisive as distinct from hesitant step in that direction. The state is now interfering in education in Britain because it believes that it has no choice but to do so. The reason is said to be parental and public anxiety about low standards. But anxiety about low standards bears the same relationship to the real cause of greater state control as the shots at Sarajevo bear to the real causes of the First World War. Parental anxiety is the excuse; the real motivation is Britain's belated recognition that economic prosperity and education are closely linked.

That points the way to my second question but I want to tie up the loose ends on the first. How far should education be geared to the needs of the state?

In the anglo-saxon world we have been conditioned to think that liberal education is good and state controlled education is bad. But in the wider historical and international perspective, that value judgment looks simplistic. An education system entirely free from state control is a luxury that few countries can afford. A developing country in need of specific skills cannot allow its schools and universities to teach what they like; it has a duty to exercise the degree of control over education that will produce the skills that are needed. The same principle applies to Britain or indeed to any other country. Governments that allow education to go its own way when the country needs a better educated workforce are just as irresponsible as governments that ignore national defence.

I am not in favour of unlimited state control of education but that is not an issue that worries me because I know that in a democracy the limit will be set by parliament. Nor am I in favour of an education system that does not encourage pupils to think for themselves because such a system would in the end undermine democracy. But we need to keep the dangers of state direction in perspective. A national curriculum does *not* stop pupils learning to think for themselves any more than giving extra money to university departments that are thought to be economically useful is a curtailment of academic freedom. Nor should we persuade ourselves that a liberal education produced lots of young men and women with independent minds. The idea that if only the government would leave schools to their own devises, the teachers and the pupils would engage in a series of Socratic dialogues is obvious nonsense. When critics of state control argue that it ignores the interests of the individual, they forget that under the free-for-all that was British education before 1988, most individuals received such a bad education they were qualified for nothing but the most unskilled jobs.

You will gather that I am an advocate of state control of education within the limits that can be set by a democracy (resisting political indoctrination for example). I am glad Britain has at last accepted the need for state intervention in education. Whether Britain has gone about it in the right way depends on the answer to my second question.

What is the Connection Between Education and Economic Prosperity?

If you have an agricultural economy you do not need an educated work force. In the first stages of industrialisation you can get away with an undereducated population because the manufacture of goods still depends primarily on human sinew. As manufacturing becomes more dependent on technology you need a work force that has at least an elementary education. When you reach the age of high technology—then you will not survive let alone compete unless your work force is well educated, unless you gave a high level of education across the population. A well educated elite and an undereducated mass is a formula for economic decline.

There is no secret about all this; it has been known for centuries. In the 17th century we find Cardinal Richelieu talking like Kenneth Baker opening the first City Technology College: 'the commerce of letters would drive out that of good from which the wealth of the state is derived ... It is for this reason that statesmen in a well-run country would wish to have as teachers more masters of mechanic arts than of liberal arts'.

But it is not enough to know that there is a connection between education and economic prosperity; you have to know too what the implications are and act upon that knowledge. Britain was quite clear about the connection and its implications over a hundred years ago. When W.E. Forster introduced the first Education Act in 1870 he put the connection clearly to the House of Commons:

> 'Upon the speedy provision of elementary education depends our industrial prosperity. It is no use trying to give technical teaching to our artisans without elementary education; uneducated labourers are for the most part unskilled labourers, and if we have our workfolk any longer unskilled, notwithstanding their strong sinews and determined energy, they will become overmatched in the competition of the world.'

A few years later, a Royal Commission on Technical Education visited schools in Germany and reported: 'The one point in which

Germany is overwhelmingly superior to England is in schools and in the education of all classes of people. The dense ignorance so common among workmen in England is unknown...'

The message was clear. Germany is already overtaking you as an industrial power and its success is based on the quality of education it provides for all classes. But 100 years later Britain had still not acted on the implications of what W.E. Forster and the Royal Commission had told them. The reasons for the delay are too well known to require elaboration. The anti-industrial bias in British society and particularly in British education (not least in its most prestigious independent schools) has been fully exposed, notably by Correlli Barnett and Martin J. Wiener.[1] Just as harmful was Britian's continuing delusion of grandeur: in 1945, Britain was a victor, still one of the big three at Potsdam and still in possession of a world-wide empire. Gearing the education system to the economic needs of the state seemed as unnecessary as it was unthinkable.

In 1988, it appears, the British have got the message. The Education Reform Act, whatever its critics might say, does aim both to direct the content and raise the standard of British education. Whether, however, the British have understood the message correctly is less clear and it is to clarifying this point that I want to devote the rest of this paper.

Britain has adopted a degree of state direction of education for economic reasons whatever the public rhetoric about parents and standards. The relevance of the measures Britain has taken must be judged therefore by how much they will enable the country to compete with the economic high-flyers. The economic high-flyer, as we are no doubt tired of hearing, is Japan. Attempts to translate Japan's education system into western terms can be misleading because there are cultural factors that do not travel. But the connection between education and economic success in Japan has lessons that can be universally applied.

The principal lesson of Japanese economic success is that it is based on a population which has a high level of general (as distinct from specialized or vocational) education. If we look at the education of Japanese young people up to the age of 18 we find: (a) that the vast majority—95 per cent—are still in full time education at the age of 18 despite a school leaving age of 15; (b) that the education they are receiving up to 18 is general i.e. it is neither specialized in the British sense of narrowing down to 3 A level subjects at 16, nor specialized in the sense of becoming at that age vocational training. As is well known, training in Japan is largely the responsibility of the companies that students join either post-school or post-university. The school system is not geared to producing specific skills. What the insistence on general education does mean is that at 18, 95 per cent of young Japanese are studying mathematics. I calculate that at 18, only between 10 per cent and 15 per cent of young Britons are studying mathematics.

There may be aspects of the Japanese education system we do not like, such as the intense competition to get into a senior high school and university. There are also cultural aspects we cannot easily borrow, such as an attitude to hard work that most British children would regard as indecent. But to ignore the relevance of what is happening in Japanese education because intense competition produces casualties—as some commentators in Britain do—is a serious mistake.

How does Britain's reformed education scene match up to the Japanese model (and one could add the South Korean or Chinese model)?

1. The central direction of the curriculum is one positive attempt to match British education to the best of the competition. In the context of this session, there is one aspect that needs highlighting and that is the emphasis on technology. Technology is a compulsory subject in the National Curriculum; the Technical and Vocational Education Initiative (TVEI) pre-dates the new Act and the City Technology Colleges are being established in the wake of the Act. Like a hardened sinner who has seen the light, the British are determined to be seen to embrace the doctrine of technology that their education system ignored for so long. I just want to sound a cautionary note. We may need school technology to correct the cultural bias against it but the evidence that technology in schools is a key ingredient in economic success is not convincing. It is true that since the 19th century there has been a strong element of technical education in Germany and that most historians would say this was essential to that country's military and economic success. But attempts in the Soviet Union to polytechnise secondary education in the 1950s to produce the skills that were needed were far from successful; and in the modern context, Japan's school curriculum is notable for the *absence* of technology. In Japan's schools 'industrial studies' for boys are set against 'homemaking' for girls and it is clear that neither of them has a high priority.

It may be that Britain's emphasis on technology in the classroom is a response to the needs of the past not the needs of the future. When Kenneth Baker says that the advantage of technology in the National Curriculum is that 'even those who are academically gifted will have to roll up their sleeves and learn a craft' his words have a quaint, archaic ring. Learning a craft does not sound like a sufficient response to the challenge of Japan's dazzlingly successful general education.

2. Britain's reformed education has a much more serious flaw than a rather naive faith in school technology. If we wonder why the Japanese are so successful we need only look at one statistic. I mentioned that at 18, 95 per cent of Japanese are still in full time education. The most generous estimate of those in full time education at 18 gives Britain a figure of 33 per cent. The British system still positively discourages young people from remaining in education after 16. That is a legacy of our elitist tradition; there is nothing wrong with elitism if it serves your purpose but if your aim is (as it should be to produce a well-educated population) then elitism is a barrier to achieving that aim. What discourages three-quarters of British youngsters from staying at school is that the British system limits post-16 education to those deemed to be capable of the sort of academic specialization that other countries regard as suitable for undergraduate or even post-graduate study. An attempt to broaden the 16-18 curriculum was made this year in the report of a government committee (the Higginson Committee) but its recommendations were rejected by the government. That decision will delay Britain's chances of producing the well-educated population it needs in order to compete in the 21st century.

I welcome many of the reforms in the 1988 Act and the National Curriculum in particular, but I do not believe that these reforms will enable Britain's education system to match the Japanese or indeed any other education system that is clearly geared to producing the high quality work force that the era of high technology will increasingly require. Britain's problem remains exactly as W.E. Forster described in 1870, 118 years ago. We will not compete economically until we raise the overall level of education in the country. Critics talk about Britain having the 'last proletariat' in the developed world. As Director of The Laura Ashley Foundation, my job is to find ways to help individuals obtain a 'second chance' in education, to reach, if you like, those parts of the brain that the education system didn't reach. It can be exciting but it can also be profoundly depressing. Those phrases describing 19th century Britain keep coming back to me: 'the dense ignorance so common among working men in England...' One illustration. We were asked to help a literacy and numeracy scheme in one of Britain's cities. The scheme was necessary because 86 per cent of the school leavers could not complete a simple job application form correctly. After 11 years of compulsory schooling they could not even get to first base.

If we are talking about preparation for the world of work, the first thing Britain has to provide is not training but basic education. If we are talking about gearing the education system to the needs of the economy, Britain should think twice before pinning her hopes on technology in schools and vocational training for 16 to 18 year olds. It may well be that the time when those solutions would have been effective has already passed; and that the Japanese experience indicates that it is full time, non-specialized, non-vocational education for all to 18 that is the basis of economic prosperity. If that analysis is correct, Britain's education system is still in need of major reform.

Note
1. *The Collapse of British Power* 1975, and *English Culture and the Decline of the Industrial Spirit*, 1981.

II

COORDINATION VERSUS DECENTRALISATION

Centralisation or Decentralisation: Alternative Strategies for Public Policy for Universities and Colleges in Canada

DAVID M. CAMERON
   DEPARTMENT OF POLITICAL SCIENCE, DALHOUSIE UNIVERSITY
   SCHOLAR-IN-RESIDENCE, INSTITUTE FOR RESEARCH ON
   PUBLIC POLICY

Introduction

The question posed in this paper is whether universities and colleges might develop more effectively within a centralised scheme of planning and administration or a decentralised system of competing institutions. This is a question for public policy, and it must therefore seek an answer ultimately through the political process. We cannot simply force an answer from such principles as academic freedom or institutional autonomy, long the shibboleths of the university community in Canada. There just is no right or wrong answer, to be determined *a priori*, to this policy question.

   The fact that this is a question or issue for determination by government as a matter of public policy and is not predetermined by the idea of a university does not negate the fact that it is nonetheless an issue with enormous consequences for the institutions affected. It is also of considerable consequence for public policy itself, in the sense that other, more specific policy objectives may be more or less likely of accomplishment depending on the approach taken. The choice between centralisation and decentralisation thus becomes not just a policy choice, but very much a strategic one.

   Before proceeding to further consideration of this strategic issue, a word or two about its application in Canada might be useful. First of all, the issue arises only at the provincial level; there is no need to waste our time considering the unconstitutional and impractical possibility of a federal policy—centralised or decentralised—for universities and colleges.

Second, there are wide variations in the circumstances of the ten provinces, and consequently the choice made by one province may not be appropriate for another. Two provinces, for example (Newfoundland and Prince Edward Island), have only one university. On the face of it, the choice between centralisation and decentralisation, at least as these terms are described below, is an empty one where only one institution is involved. The world is seldom as simple as the face of things suggests, however. Prince Edward Island participates in the Maritime Provinces Higher Education Commission (MPHEC), a three-province buffer agency. The MPHEC has responsibility for the oversight of over twenty institutions, one of which is the University of Prince Edward Island. It is certainly open for the three provinces to use the MPHEC as an agent for either a centralised or decentralised approach, and thus a strategic choice of approach can arise even for a province with but one university.

The third, and final feature of the Canadian context worth noting at the outset is the fact that all ten provinces have now adopted some variant of a binary post-secondary system. The two sets of institutions are everywhere distinguished by the titles 'college' and 'university'. And while there is remarkable similarity in the meaning of a university in all provinces, there is wide variation in what is meant by a college. In Quebec, the *collèges d'enseignement général et professionnel* (CEGEPs) combine a two-year collegiate programme, the only route to university, with three-year terminal vocational programmes. In Ontario, by way of contrast, the Colleges of Applied Arts and Technology (CAATs) do not, as a matter of provincial policy, offer university transfer programmes of any kind, although individual universities may give some credit for college work, and the legislative door is open to specific college-university joint programming. Alberta and British Columbia offer yet another variant, where the first year or two of university work may be done in *either* a college or a university.

The strategic choice between centralisation and decentralisation arises, then, for ten provincial governments, three of which deal with their universities through a single regional buffer agency, and all of which are committed to binary post-secondary systems, albeit binary systems which vary considerably from province to province. Given this general framework, what are the properties of the two strategic approaches?

The Two Strategic Approaches

What we have thus far referred to as the centralised approach must be distinguished from direct government control and operation of universities and colleges. A few technical institutes continue to be operated this way, but the trend has clearly been in the opposite direction and most of the institutions that were once government-operated now have their own governing boards. This has not stopped some academic critics from seeing signs of provincial government intentions to establish operational control lurking behind or within specific government statements or proposals.[1] Moreover, just over a decade ago, OECD's examiners cautioned that '... some provincial authorities go too far in their attempts to control institutional decisions, particularly in Alberta and Quebec.'[2]

Centralisation without direct government control can better be described, I believe, as coordination, and it is to a further consideration of this concept that we now turn.

The Coordinative Approach

The essential feature of the coordinative approach to provincial post-secondary policy is the idea of a *system* of institutions, each with specific roles and responsibilities. It can be left to the institutions to determine how best to organise and deliver their programmes, thus preserving a substantial element of institutional autonomy, but what programmes are to be delivered is a matter for decision by a central authority.

In policy terms, such a system is driven by an overarching plan, usually referred to as the master plan for the system. This may be more or less specific, but its purpose is to structure the responsibilities, and both constrain and channel the ambitions of the constituent institutions such that they collectively serve the defined needs of the provincial post-secondary system as a whole.

In structural terms, this approach is given expression through a central coordinating agency, whose task is to formulate the master plan and to ensure that institutional developments fall within its dictates and priorities. For the latter purpose, the agency can be expected to have one or both of two principal instruments at its disposal: fiscal persuasion, exercised through the distribution of government grants, and regulatory control, exercised by means of programme review and approval. The common currency of the coordinating agency and the constituent institutions is information, invariably large volumes of information.

There are at least three models of the coordinative approach available. One places planning and administrative responsibility within a government department, incorporating the master plan in legislation, directly or through subordinate regulations. A second approach, embodying an arms-length relationship between government and institutions, places coordinating authority in the hands of a non-departmental board, council, or commission, operating under authority delegated by legislation. The third approach establishes a two-tier institutional structure, with existing institutions becoming constituent units in a 'provincial' college or university responsible for overall planning and coordination.

Canada has very little experience with the coordinative approach in the case of its universities, despite the examples of several American state systems, and at least two official proposals for its adoption.

In 1966, for example, the Spinks Report observed that 'The most striking characteristic of higher... education in Ontario is *the complete absence of a master plan, of an educational policy, and of a co-ordinating authority for the provincially-supported institutions.*' To fill that gap, the report recommended '... in the strongest terms that a Provincial University of Ontario be established.'[3]

More recently, in 1985, a royal commission in Nova Scotia recommended that 'A provincial intermediary body, called the Nova Scotia Council on Higher Education, should be established and endowed with executive authority and discretionary powers over funding in order *to ensure that university planning, programming and resource allocation are performed in the context of a provincial university system.*'[4] Moreover, the commission continued, 'should the Council on Higher Education prove inadequate to coordinate the academic programmes and expenditures of the universities, the provincial government should consider the consolidation of the separate institutions in a University of Nova Scotia.'[5]

In order to put these two proposals for provincial universities into context, it might be noted that Nova Scotia has no fewer than eleven degree-granting institutions for a population of 873,000, while Ontario has sixteen degree-granting institutions for a population of 9.1 million.[6]

Quebec actually established a variant of the coordinated provincial university when it created l'Université du Québec in 1968. This institution has its headquarters, but no campus, in the city of Quebec and constituent campus units in Montreal, Chicoutimi, Trois-Rivière, Rimouski, Hull and l'Abitibi-Témiscamingue, as well as three specialised schools and two research institutes. Indeed, it has all the markings of a provincial university, except that it is only one among the seven universities which constitute the Quebec system.

While the coordinative approach remains for the most part foreign to Canada's university sector, it has been the common approach in the case of colleges. In New Brunswick, for example, the college system was established as a single corporate entity, The New Brunswick Community College. The same model was followed in Nova Scotia in 1986-87 when it became the tenth province to establish a college system, creating the Nova Scotia Community College with sixteen constituent campus units. In Ontario, a provincial Council of Regents was given wide-ranging authority, including approval of programmes and management responsibility for province-wide collective bargaining, with respect to the board-operated CAATs.

It is interesting to note, however, that this very centralisation of authority in the college sector has been subject to growing criticism. In his recent review of the governance of Ontario's CAATs, for example, undertaken for the Minister of Colleges and Universities in the aftermath of a traumatic province-wide faculty strike, Walter Pitman concluded that '... the current Council of Regents, with its executive powers, can no longer be sustained.' The Council, he argued, should be advisory only, and '... executive authority ... should devolve on the local college or, where necessary, on the Minister.'[7] The Government of Ontario appears to be heeding this advice.

We thus encounter the alternative to centralisation, redefined as coordination, in the form of decentralisation. And with that, we must immediately distinguish between the devolution of responsibility for post-secondary education to private institutions, and competition between public institutions within bounds prescribed by public policy. The first of these can better be described as a policy of privatisation. Canada's universities and colleges are virtually all public institutions, in fact if not always in their legal foundations. It is therefore only the second approach to decentralisation that is practical, one that I think can better be described as the competitive approach to public policy.[8]

The Competitive Approach

The key feature of this approach is the scope granted to institutions to pursue their individual strategic advantages. The focus of public policy is not on control and direction, but rather on preserving a competitive environment and ensuring that incentives are in place sufficient to attract institutional responses to public policy objectives. Institutions have substantial freedom to devise their own mix of programmes, to set their own tuition, and to set and pursue their strategic objectives, but within a framework of rules and incentives prescribed at the provincial level.

In policy terms, planning is just as important in the competitive approach, but the nature of planning is quite different. At the provincial level, the approach is likely to be more sectoral than comprehensive, addressing specific programme priorities rather than the system as a whole. At the local level, planning becomes more strategic, for each institution must define its own role and priorities within the provincial system.

In structural terms, the competitive approach is equally dependent on a provincial, or intermediate agency. The task of such an agency is to set the bounds of institutional competition (for example, the range within which tuition fees may vary) and also to ensure that incentives are in place sufficient to call forth institutional responses to provincial priorities. In terms of instruments, fiscal incentives loom large. Less emphasis is likely to be placed on programme review and approval as a regulatory process. Rather, the process itself becomes competitive with institutions bidding for approval and funding of new programmes called for by the province, and with the province free to withdraw funding from programmes or areas deemed redundant.

The latter point warrants at least brief elaboration, for it nicely encapsulates the fundamental difference between the two approaches. In a situation where the provincial government has determined, for example, that the number of, say, physical education programmes should be reduced by one (say from four to three), it might simply invite the institutions currently offering physical education to make their cases for continuing their programmes. On the basis of this information, it could then determine which three programmes to fund. The weakest of the four would lose, or at least the one making the weakest case would lose. The same principle would apply just as well in reverse. Where new programmes are to be funded, institutions might be invited to submit proposals. In this case, the strongest proposal would carry the day.

The most obvious illustration of the competitive approach in Canada is the funding of university-based research. Here, most of the funds covering the direct costs of research come from the federal government, with individual researchers or groups of researchers bidding for the available funding on the basis of peer-adjudicated submissions and proposals. Determination of the research categories to be supported, the allocation of funds between them, and the administration of the competition is the responsibility of the three federal granting councils. As reorganised in 1978, these are the Medical Research Council (MRC), the Natural Sciences and Engineering Research Council (NSERC), and the Social Sciences and Humanities Research Council (SSHRC).

The significance of the research example is seen in the fact that universities, as institutions, succeed or fail in the competition for research dollars on the basis of the performance of their researchers. Institutions are not designated as research-intensive, and therefore more heavily funded for research, as might be expected under the coordinative approach. Rather, institutions *become* research-intensive by virtue of their successful competition for research funds.

The major flaw in the present system of funding research in Canada is the limitation of federal research grants to the direct costs of the project, excluding overhead or indirect costs, and in most cases even the salaries of the principal investigators. These become charges on the operating budget of the university concerned, and therefore on provincial operating grants. The latter, however, are not sensitive to research expenditures, with the paradoxical consequence that universities are actually penalised financially for the success of their researchers in attracting funds.

Several provinces, and now the federal government, have recently added a different approach to funding research, although still a competitive one. Research centres, rather than individual projects and researchers, are being supported over a number of years as centres of excellence or centres of specialisation.

There is much to be said for this approach, not only because of the more comprehensive funding involved, but also because of the scope for the formation of multi-institutional consortiums or networks. The latter has the added potential of facilitating the work of strong researchers in small or relatively weak institutions, by allowing them to be associated with a centre of excellence but without necessarily relocating on a permanent basis.

The major concern is whether the approach will remain truly competitive, or whether the substantial sums involved will invite partisan political considerations and institutional lobbying, the Achilles' heel of the competitive approach. Thus far, Canada's track record has been reasonable, and plans for the new 'centres of excellence' programme are promising. There have been cases in the past, however, where the allocative process has been little short of scandalous from a serious research perspective.[9]

Beginning in 1967 the federal government sought to employ a competitive approach in the purchase of job-related training from provincial colleges and technical institutes. Ontario, in particular, was successful in interposing itself as exclusive broker, frustrating the federal attempt at dealing directly with its newly-established colleges.[10] More recently, the federal government has shifted the focus of its funding to the private sector in a continuing effort to escape being captured by provincial and institutional priorities. Indeed, even the provinces frequently find it advantageous to separate responsibility for the regulation and financing of institutions from the promotion of specific training and research objectives. Ontario, for example, has placed responsibility for job training and research in ministries other than Colleges and Universities. This brings us to the question of whether coordination or competition is more likely to promote change and enhance institutional adaptability.

Change and Adaptability

There is real concern in Canada that our post-secondary institutions, and especially our universities, have become excessively rigid organisations. The basis for this rigidity lies in two directions, I believe.

First, provincial policy has, since the 1950s, been devoted to the objective of accessibility and, since the 1970s, of expenditure restraint as well. This has led to the imposition of a number of constraints on independent action by university boards. Tuition, for example, has been effectively controlled by provincial governments in the name of access, whether by legislation, financial administration, or political suasion. Similarly, the introduction of new programmes has been constrained as a means of expenditure control.

Second, even greater constraints have arisen internally. The Duff-Berhahl report[11] opened the flood-gates of democratic management. Faculty unionisation, now characteristic of most universities whether on a voluntary basis or, more frequently, under provincial trade union legislation, has both cemented an employer-employee relationship and further constrained institutional capacity to make staff changes in response to programme or financial pressures (let alone redundancy or exigency). The result is a university system whose academic staff complement is fixed, aging, and able to block programme changes. For their part, universities have at best only limited capacities to formulate priorities.

Canada's colleges have traditionally had greater programme flexibility, reflecting their economic rationale and more specific job-related training responsibilities. In large part, however, this was established with the heavy hand of provincial regulatory control, which has exacted its own price in terms of staff morale and student preferences. It is worth noting that considerable pressure is developing to establish a more 'collegial' atmosphere in the colleges, and thus to take on more of the organisational attributes of universities.

The fact of the matter is that in both sectors there is real concern that we have not been able to sustain public institutions that are sufficiently responsive to changing external demands while at the same time retaining a dynamic internal culture that fosters creativity and high standards.

Does a solution lie in placing more emphasis in provincial policy on coordination (centralisation) or competition (decentralisation)? Frankly, I think there is much to be said for increased competition. It seems to me that it is the element of competition, based on peer adjudication, that has kept our research enterprise remarkably vibrant, even in the face of stagnant funding and in rather sharp contrast to the moribund status of many undergraduate programmes.

Increased competition is not synonymous with a market-driven, laissez faire approach (earlier defined as privatisation). Institutions would be expected to be more responsive to external demands, but not randomly so, and not to all demands. As public institutions, universities and colleges would be expected to respond to demands generated or interpreted by public policy. Formulation of the latter would be the responsibility of a public agency, department or commission.

An intermediary agency is thus just as appropriate, and perhaps as essential under a competitive approach as under a coordinative one. Its tasks are quite different, however. In a competitive approach, the province must define the objectives and priorities of public policy for post-secondary education as surely as in a coordinative approach, but it then puts in place incentives, rather than regulations, sufficient to call forth appropriate institutional responses. The question then comes down to whether regulations or incentives are the more effective instrument. Where a principal objective is enhanced institutional adaptability, it is difficult to conclude otherwise than that incentives are more likely to prove effective.

This will not occur automatically, however. In addition to the need for a clearer enunciation of public policy objectives and priorities, there appear to be two critical conditions for success.

Conditions for Effective Competition

The first condition is probably the most difficult. It is that provincial governments resist the temptation to accede to community or institutional pressures to compensate the losers in the competitive process or, worse still, to manipulate the rules to favour weaker applicants. The competitive approach is attractive precisely because it rewards superior performance; it rewards the winners.

The task is to enhance the capacity for institutional strategic planning so that comparative advantages can be identified and pursued within each institution. It would be the ultimate in poor management if an institution were unable to 'win' in any areas at all.

This immediately points to the second condition for workable competition. For institutions to engage in strategic planning, there must be a governing authority capable not only of taking a comprehensive view of the institution's strengths and weaknesses in relation to external demands and opportunities, but also of taking decisions. This governing authority must be able to make choices among and between programmes in which members of the institution have vested interests, and sometimes strong professional interests. It is precisely such choices which elude representative senates and their equivalent.

This is where the role of the lay board of governors becomes critical. Yet the combination of provincial policy constraints and faculty unionisation has had the effect of squeezing from boards much of their governing authority. The authority of boards must be secured and, where necessary, reestablished. But boards are in no position actually to manage universities or colleges. Indeed, their responsibility is not to manage the institution, but to ensure that it is well managed.

Among the specific tasks falling to governing boards, a commitment to strategic planning would come at the top of virtually any list. Again, it should be emphasised that the board itself need not necessarily do the planning; it must, however, insist that it is done. More than that, it must see that it is done well (meaning that it is more than a process of confirming what the institution is already doing), and that it has an impact on subsequent decisions. Boards might also be more concerned than many are with evaluation—of programmes, of management systems, and of personnel. In some cases, the membership of boards may require attention if they are to justify the public trust implicit in a strengthened role.

But when all is said and done, there is probably no more important or effective place to start the reform of post-secondary education in Canada than by strengthening the governing boards of universities and colleges. Within the context of a more competitive, or decentralised, approach to public policy, stronger boards may be the key to promoting dynamic, adaptive institutions, capable of identifying and pursuing their comparative advantages.

Notes

1. See, for example, Ian Winchester, 'Government Power and University Principles: An Analysis of the Battle for Academic Freedom in Alberta' in Winchester, ed., *The Independence of the University and the Funding of the State: Essays on Academic Freedom in Canada.* Toronto: OISE Press (Special theme issue of *Interchange*), 1984.

2. OECD, *Reviews of National Policies for Education: Canada*. Paris: OECD, 1976, p. 82.

3. Ontario, Commission to Study the Development of Graduate Programmes in Ontario Universities, *Report*. Toronto: Committee on University Affairs and Committee of Presidents of Provincially-Assisted Universities, 1966, pp. 77-80. Emphasis added.

4. Nova Scotia, Royal Commission on Post-Secondary Education, *Report*. Halifax: Queen's Printer, 1985, p. 175. Emphasis added.

5. Ibid., p. 178.

6. Counting and categorising post-secondary institutions is notoriously difficult. Excluded from these numbers are institutions whose degree-granting powers are held in abeyance or exercised through another institution.

7. Walter Pitman, *Report of the Advisor to the Minister of Colleges and Universities on the Governance of the Colleges of Applied Arts and Technology*. Toronto: Ministry of Colleges and Universities, 1966, p. 22.

8. I am indebted to Dr. Ron Watts, of Queen's University, for the distinction between 'coordination' and 'competition' as alternative approaches to public policy. My debt is gratefully acknowledged.

9. Perhaps the most glaring instance occurred with the $25 million 'Centre of Specialisation Program' of the federal Secretary of State in 1983-84.

10. See J. Stefan Dupré, et al., *Federalism and Policy Development: The Case of Adult Occupational Training in Ontario*. Toronto: University of Toronto Press, 1973.

11. *University Government in Canada*. Report of a Commission sponsored by the Canadian Association of University Teachers and the Association of Universities and Colleges of Canada (Sir James Duff and Prof. Robert Berdahl, Commissioners). Toronto: University of Toronto Press, 1966.

The Struggle for Higher Education Resources

RALPH G. M. SULTAN, PRESIDENT, NORTHERN INVESTORS INC.
PAUL E. SULTAN, PROFESSOR, UNIVERSITY OF ILLINOIS

In his essay *The Future of the Universities* Ron L. Watts (1983) observed that universities face a period of dramatic change. He asked whether these most conservative of institutions could adapt rapidly enough to survive the very conditions they had created. He was referring to the role universities now play in economic development, more particularly their creation of knowledge, science and technology.

Watt's forecast was accurate; massive exogenous forces are playing upon the university. The commercialization of what we call 'knowledge' is accelerating. Scholars are no longer viewed as eccentric passengers on the train of growth; they are seen as its engine. Universities are being lured from their sanctuary on the hill into the hurly burly of the marketplace; or, more accurately, the hurly burly is enveloping the groves of academe.

What will happen to the traditional concept of the university is the unanswered question. The emerging institution will certainly differ from the current model. And the resource base of the university—its manner of funding—will determine significantly its degrees of freedom. We believe the universities' key to survival as independent institutions lies in ample funding and diversified funding. This essay is concerned with how to achieve those objectives.

Public policy acknowledges the economic potential of the university, but has not come to grips with the resources issue. How much should a nation spend on higher education? Is government to remain the primary funder of higher education? Is the level of resources committed by government adequate? What should be the form of payment?

In considering these issues it is helpful to draw some international comparisons. How are Canada and the United Kingdom faring in comparison with such economic rivals as Japan and the United States?

International Resource Comparisons
Share of GNP

First consider the magnitude of national commitment to education spending at all levels. According to the most recent available UNESCO data (Table 1) Canada and the Soviet Union are spending the largest percentage of their Gross National Product on education, closely followed by the United States. Japan and the United Kingdom lag noticeably behind.

Table 1
Percentage of Gross National Product Allocated
to Total Education Expenditures

	1975	1983-1985
Canada	7.6%	7.0%
Soviet Union	7.6	7.0
United States	6.3	6.7
United Kingdom	6.7	5.2
Japan	5.5	5.1

Source: UNESCO, *Yearbook of Education Statistics*, Nancy, France: Imprimerie Berger Leurault, 1980 and 1988.

Where are these education dollars being concentrated? Again, according to UNESCO data (Table 2) the United States is spending a comparatively large proportion of its total education budget (37 per cent) on post-secondary education. Furthermore, the American proportion of national income consumed by higher education seems to be rising. This is not a universal strategy. Japan and the Soviet Union appear to be concentrating 80 per cent to 90 per cent of their national educational resources at the primary and secondary level.

Table 2
Post-Secondary Education as a Percentage of Gross National Product as a Percentage of Total Education Spending

	% Share of GNP 1975	% Share of GNP 1983-85	% Share of Education 1983-85
United States	2.0%	2.5%	37.0%
Canada	2.2	2.0	29.0
United Kingdom	1.4	1.1	21.0
Soviet Union	1.0	0.9	13.0
Japan	0.6	0.5	10.0

Source: Derived from UNESCO data.

Given the range and depth of its institutions, we are not surprised to see the United States clearly ahead of other major countries in the percentage of its Gross National Product (2.5 per cent) devoted to higher education. It is more astonishing to see economic arch-rival Japan ranked at the very bottom of this short list (0.5 per cent of GNP). Whatever national economic success we may attribute to the intensive Japanese educational experience, and whatever competitive weakness we may attribute to our own, these do not in the first instance seem to correlate with the proportion of GNP being spent on higher education. Simply spending more money at the university level guarantees neither educational distinction nor economic prowess. At the same time, there is no denying that the level of resources fed into higher education is a major determinant of the quality of higher education coming out, regardless of country. In this respect, the vaunted Japanese educational system does its best work **before** the students arrive at university, and one is entitled to question the depth and calibre of the Japanese university system itself.

There is a suggestion that (with the exception of the United States) the share of national resources committed to **post-secondary** education has been *dropping* in various countries, including Canada and the United Kingdom. This is consistent with other data, and supports our hypothesis that in countries with predominantly government-financed university systems, such as Canada and the United Kingdom, the emergence of other political priorities such as social security and medical care has eroded government commitment to higher education. We suspect that a resource allocation sensitive to political considerations will increasingly favour the aged over the young; university students have fewer votes. Only in the more market-oriented United States higher education system has spending on higher education grown faster than the economy as a whole.

As one ponders these statistics, other provocative hypotheses emerge: perhaps the expanding American educational resources are being committed at the wrong level, in a futile endeavour to build edifices of higher learning on a crumbling primary and secondary education foundation. Higher education is not easily grafted upon illiterates. Perhaps the American educational system shares certain traits with its health delivery system, where higher prices and higher expenditures do not necessarily lead to a healthier (read: 'better educated') population. If elite American universities simply escalate their tuition prices to exploit an inelastic demand, does this improve the quantity or quality of education, when viewed as a national resource? We think not, and such considerations must be weighed in public policy concerning the future funding mechanism of higher education.

Participation and Penetration

Another measure of a nation's resource commitment to higher education is the market penetration achieved: what proportion of the population participates? This is a measure of investment, for income foregone by individuals is a major component of any nation's cost of higher education. Let us therefore consider the proportion of citizens investing in higher education.

The annual output of university graduates, expressed as a percentage of the total population, is highest for the United States (0.62 per cent), considerably lower in the case of Canada (.47 per cent) and Japan (0.43 per cent), and lowest for the United Kingdom (0.28 per cent). (Watts 1987).

Similar conclusions obtain when we compare the percentage of population enrolled in post-secondary education (Table 3). It is clear that the United States and Canada have achieved a level of higher educational penetration—more than double that of other key international competitors, including Japan. The United Kingdom lags far behind. If mere attendance was the most important criterion, North America would seem well positioned to win any competitive struggle against other nations in the knowledge industries. In similar vein, one would be prompted to wonder about the long-term economic prospects of the United Kingdom.

Table 3
**Percentage of Total Population
in Higher Education Attendance**

	1975	1985
United States	5.1%	5.1%
Canada	3.6	5.1
Japan	2.0	2.0
Soviet Union	1.9	1.9
United Kingdom	1.3	1.8

Source: UNESCO, *Yearbook of Education Statistics*, Nancy, France: Imprimerie Berger Leurault, 1980 and 1988. Includes both full-time and part-time students, enrolled at universities, technical institutes, and two-year and three-year colleges.

These international rankings are replicated when we examine statistics on attendance at colleges and universities only (as opposed to all post-secondary institutions); and when we examine the percentage of the age 20 to 24 age cohort, both full-time and part-time, which is enroled in some form of higher education (UNESCO 1988).

It is clear that the current economic success being enjoyed by Japan cannot be correlated in any simple fashion to superiority in numbers of students on Japanese campuses. We are driven to the obvious conclusion that what is learned and the discipline of the process are at least as important as sheer numbers of students. For example, Canadian and American mass higher education probably contributes little to economic growth and competitiveness when it focuses on the production of lawyers in lieu of engineers.

We also note significant international variations in the 'mix' of higher education, as between universities and colleges on the one hand, and other post-secondary institutions such as technical institutes on the other (Table 4).

There are great problems of definition here, but comparatively speaking, it seems safe to conclude that the United Kingdom in particular, followed by Canada, tends to favour 'other' forms of higher education in lieu of universities. It is conceivable that we witness in Canada the fading remnants of a British tradition of apprenticeship and trade schools for the masses and of university reserved for the elite.

Table 4
Percentage of Total Population in Higher Education Attendance

	Universities and Colleges	Other Post-Secondary
Canada	3.0%	2.2%
United States	3.2	1.9
United Kingdom	0.6	1.0
Japan	1.6	0.4

Source: UNESCO, *Yearbook of Education Statistics*, Nancy, France: Imprimerie Berger Leurault, 1980 and 1988.

Resources per Student

Consider next the per-student intensity of resource commitment in higher education. Are resources lavished on the few, or spread more thinly (more efficiently?) over the many? Since one particularly important resource is staff, a key measure of resource intensity is the ratio of faculty to students (Table 5).

One concludes that Canada is **very** lean in terms of teaching resources per student, and that the United States is fairly lean in comparison with Japan and the Soviet Union, which are overstaffed by comparison. Others may wish to examine whether these are not simply indicators of institutional efficiency. Our own hypothesis is that North American institutions of higher learning, under competitive pressure, tend to fill up their classrooms and limit small seminars, thereby causing relatively high student-faculty ratios. North American frugality in per-student resources might appear more exaggerated if one could account for the percentage of faculty time consumed by research as opposed to teaching.

A final indicator of resource intensity may be obtained by computing the share of GNP divided by the share of population in higher education (Table 6). The implied share of national resources commanded **per student** in the United Kingdom is startling—surpassing even that of the United States. Japan appears at the other extreme, in its apparent unwillingness to concentrate a large share of national income **per student** in higher education.

Table 5
Ratio of Students to Faculty All Post-Secondary Institutions

	Faculty (000)	Students (000)	Ratio
Canada	57	1,294	22.5
United States	694	12,247	17.6
Soviet Union	377	5,147	13.6
United Kingdom	79	1,006	12.7
Japan	243	2,397	9.8

Sources: UNESCO, *Yearbook of Education Statistics*, Nancy, France: Imprimerie Berger Leurault, 1980 and 1988;
Statistics Canada, *Education in Canada*, 1986-1988, Ottawa;
US Department of Education, *Digest of Education Statistics 1987*, USGPO, Washington, 1988;
United Kingdom, University Grants Committee, *Statistical Report*, London, 1988.
The above data include junior and community colleges, technical institutes, and distance education. Includes both full and part-time students and instructors.

Table 6
Index of National Resources per Student Enrolled
(Ratio: Percentage of GNP Devoted to Post-Secondary Education, divided by Percentage of Population Enrolled in Post-Secondary Education)

United Kingdom	.61
United States	.49
Soviet Union	.47
Canada	.39
Japan	.25

Source: Calculations by the authors.

Different resource intensity strategies are clearly evident. The United Kingdom appears to pursue a strategy of committing higher education resources on a generous scale *per student,* while admitting *few students.* To use an analogy, if transportation problems could be solved by putting a few more Rolls Royce automobiles on the road, the British might have an effective strategy. However, it seems that the demands of economic growth require mass transit as well as the occasional Rolls Royce. The British seem to have embraced the aphorism of Kingsly Amis: 'More is worse!'

The Role of Government Funding

Let us complete our international comparisons by examining the extent of government funding in various university systems (Table 7). The United Kingdom stands with the Soviet Union and the elite Japanese public universities, in terms of the dominant role of government finance, it being in the range of 85 per cent to 100 per cent.

At the other extreme are the private universities of the United States and Japan, which rely upon government funding for only 15 to 25 per cent of their budget. Canada's universities, with about 75 per cent government funding, occupy what might be termed a left-of-centre position on the international scale. (All of these estimates exclude government-financed student loans.)

For over a decade now, government fiscal support of higher education has been tightly constrained in most countries. A further hazard of government funding has been illustrated in the United Kingdom, where 'civil servants have become more confident of (their) ability to direct universities into 'socially desirable' directions, and more demanding of their right to do so. Parliament has accepted the belief that universities should be instruments of social policy, and held accountable to the government. As a result, the autonomy of British universities has been broken into at many points'. (Shils 1982)

Government clearly has important funding responsibilities in the field of higher education. However, the authors become concerned when government's percentage stake rises much above 50 per cent, for at that point university autonomy surely diminishes. In their future funding, universities must now develop a fine balancing act between the heavy hand of government interference on the one hand, and the opportunistic mayhem of the marketplace on the other.

Table 7
Estimated Source of University Income

	Government	Non-Government (including tuition fees regardless of source)	
Canada	75%	25%	(authors' est.)
United States			
Private	25%	75%	(U.S.D. Ed. 1988)
Public	50%	50%	(authors' est.)
Japan			
Private	15%	85%	(Ichikawa 1979)
Public	96%	4%	(Ichikawa 1979)
United Kingdom	90%	10%	(Allington 1989)
Soviet Union	100%	0%	(Shipler 1984)

The Struggle for Canadian Higher Education Resources

Canadian higher education provides an interesting case study in how the source of financial support can be gradually diversified from the government to the private arena. As we have seen, by international standards Canadian higher education has achieved a very high market penetration, but is characterized by low per-student resources and a declining share of gross national product. It is also highly dependent on government.

In recent years the Canadian university system has relied upon direct government grants for about 58 per cent of its budget, and government-sponsored research for approximately another 17 per cent of its budget, for a total of 75 per cent governmental funding from these two sources alone. Tuition income from students represented barely 12 per cent of the national university budget; endowment and investment income only 3 to 4 per cent; and alumni and other gifts scarcely more than 2 per cent of the budget. The cash drain imposed upon both Federal and Provincial Governments by the university system has been substantial, with the federal government (once the rhetoric and accounting underbrush has been cleared away) paying as much as two-thirds of the total.

Government's dominance of Canadian university finance is a post-World War II phenomenon; a legacy of the universities' desire to perpetuate a surge of revenues brought onto Canadian campuses by returning (and government-financed) war veterans. Subsequently, for fifteen years or so, the university budgets luxuriated on an expanding wave of political support. But all of that has changed. Once on the government payroll, Canadian universities have not quite figured out how to get off. Furthermore, it is not clear that government bureaucrats want to let them off.

The Canadian university resource problem may be summarized as follows:

- Inadequate funding. For about fifteen years, Canadian university budgets have been squeezed by their government patrons. Today, the Canadian universities' level of funding is clearly inadequate to the challenges the national economy has imposed. In Ontario, funding (ex-inflation) has risen by 2 or 3 per cent over a decade when student enrolment has virtually doubled.

- Too exposed to political influence. Because of the dominance of taxpayer-funding, politicians (such as the Attorney General of Ontario) make it quite clear that it is the government's responsibility to ensure that university funds are well spent. In such an environment it is no surprise to see new university research programmes (e.g., for AIDS) announced from the floor of the legislature rather than the office of the dean.

- Universities do not extract sufficient money from their primary beneficiaries, the students. Tuition at world-famous McGill University is approximately $500 US, or approximately 3 per cent of the tuition fee charged by its Ivy League competitors! In Ontario and Quebec, governments control tuition fees and refuse to raise them for fear of student backlash.

- The resource system does not reward excellence. Government grants are influenced by all-university committees that do not encourage competition. Governments tend to allocate funds on the basis of dollars per student enrolled, regardless of quality.

- The resource system encourages neither private philanthropy nor the accumulation of capital resources. Harvard University has about four times the capital endowment of all Canadian universities combined. After decades of government funding,

Canadian universities have lost much of their incentive, their organization, and their technology (e.g., data banks) for the most elementary private fund-raising.

Alternative-Funding Strategies: The Japanese Model

The financing strategy of Japanese higher education is characterized by high unit expenditures in the public university sector to ensure quality and elite education for the few (about 20 to 25 per cent of college students); while relying upon low unit expenditures in the private university sector (accounting for about 75 to 80 per cent of students) so as to achieve mass market penetration economically.

Indicative of the relative poverty of the Japanese private university is the fact that almost half of total expenditures in higher education were accounted for by the government university sector in 1976, despite its accommodating less than one-quarter of the students. Public university per-student expenditures were estimated to be 270 per cent higher than in private universities. Another indicator was the student-teacher ratio: 8.5 in the public sector and 29.5 in the private (Ichikawa 1979).

The economics of sending a child to a strictly private Japanese university would seem familiar to the parents of any Ivy League student. Tuition levels at private Japanese universities are three to four times the tuition level at government universities. In addition, private students in select fields such as medicine were obliged to contribute 'donations' several times larger than their tuition fees. Annual costs in the range of $40,000 to $50,000 US are not unusual. Enrolment in private universities has come to be skewed toward the higher-income families (Ichikawa 1979).

The Japanese model illustrates the possibilities, and the drawbacks, of a privately funded, mass-enrolment university system. Even in Japan, significant government assistance has been necessary. One might also question the fairness of taxpayer sponsorship of elitist institutions, but this is probably preferable to a system where elites are trained according to their ability to pay.

Alternative-Funding Strategies: The United States Model

United States funding of higher education is the exact opposite of the Japanese structure. American elite, resource-intensive universities are (mostly) privately funded, whereas American mass-enrolment institutions are (mostly) publicly funded. The American system can also claim a disproportionate share of the world's truly elite research universities (Rosovsky 1987). It educates the largest percentage of the population, commands the largest share of GNP and, among the countries examined, seems to be the only system which has attracted a growing as opposed to diminishing share of national product. These attributes probably derive from its highly competitive industrial structure, in contrast with the more oligopolistic or monopolistic (state-sponsored) systems of many other countries.

The United States also offers the most advanced and variegated mechanisms for the financing of higher education, an unprecedented integration of the human and financial capital markets. But even in the United States, budget crunches have necessitated fresh ideas for university funding. Many of these fresh ideas put more responsibility for education costs on the shoulders of the student. The rationale for such an approach was enunciated by US Secretary of Education William Bennett:

> The college graduate will earn $640,000 more than the high school graduate over his lifetime, an income gain of almost 53 per cent.... It is only sensible—and only fair—that the beneficiary pay the cost rather than the taxpayers, the majority of whom do not themselves enjoy the financial rewards of a college education (Vobejda 1986, p.A4).

There is probably a side benefit as well: once students pay a larger share of their costs they become more sensitive to what they are receiving for their investment; more mindful of the benefit/cost ratio of each class. That sensitivity, in the authors' own broad experience, is efficiently transmitted to faculty. Thus, higher tuition fees can be justified by the theory of consumer sovereignty.

Four-year tuition costs at such elite private schools as MIT, Yale and Stanford are in the $75,000 US range and climbing. For American public universities such costs range from $20,000 to $40,000 US for four years. Projected tuition costs for the year 2000 are in the $100,000 US range.

The parallel growth of student indebtedness is remarkable. In the past fifteen years, the US Federal Guaranteed Student Loan Program has mushroomed from $1 billion to $8.2 billion in assets under administration. The number of borrowers (one million in 1970) has increased to 3.6 million—about one-third of the total college student population. Average debt after four years now stands at $9,000 for borrowers at private colleges, and $6,700 for those attending public colleges. Students in graduate and professional schools often accumulate debts in the five-digit range, albeit in anticipation of six-digit annual earnings (Evangelauf 1987).

Meanwhile, university costs (and tuition fees) have been increasing at double the general inflation rate of the economy. Some blame runaway university costs on the broad availability of student loans that are generously subsidized by the federal government. But the current inflation is merely a continuation of longer-term tendencies; in constant-dollar terms **per-student costs** (at all levels) in the American education system have risen five-fold in 50 years (Williams 1985).

Concern about student indebtedness is not centred exclusively on the large liabilities that students carry with them as they enter the professional and technical world: debt obligations may also inhibit choice of critical occupations such as teaching that pay modestly.

Some American solutions to the funding predicament are as follows:

a. Prefunding University Costs

One major initiative involves setting up early investments for children—even infants—that can mature into a generous endowment by the time they reach college age. This plan, frequently called 'tuition futures', is actually a long-term prepayment plan.

Individual universities have tuition futures plans largely targeted at alumni, on the assumption that alumni hope their children can replicate their own educational experience. More than 250 colleges now have such plans in operation. Most of the plans build on the assumption that investment returns to the trust fund will not be taxable so long as they are not accessed by parents, and are reinvested in the fund. However, there are obvious problems: a college may not maintain its quality and may not match student choice.

To address some of these concerns, the State of Michigan has created a state-sponsored trust fund. If new parents deposit as little as $3,000, or offer regular future payments, attendance at a Michigan state college is assured. Universities have the option of refusing students who lack adequate qualification. In that event, the original principal—but not the accumulated income and capital gains—is returned to the family (Hull 1987, Hauptman 1986, Bowen, 1986).

In Canada, mutual fund companies offer similar tax-exempt Educational Savings Plans, sold to parents and grandparents. In one plan, all income and capital gains are allocated to those plan beneficiaries who actually attend college, at the expense of those who do not. The plan is quite successful, perhaps because of the strong incentive to attend college or lose!

b. Income-Contingent Loans

Another innovation in American university funding is the income-contingent student loan which calibrates repayment to income earned after graduation. In its pilot form, ten universities have offered $600 million of income-contingent loans of up to $17,500 over a four-year period. Borrowers repay at the rate of 15 per cent of income. Participating institutions have complained about the complexities of checking graduates' incomes and adjusting payments annually (Wilson 1987, Davidson 1986).

Milton Friedman proposed a national income-contingent funding institution that would draw its capitalization from the federal treasury, or as some have suggested, through sale of bonds. Provision could be made for reduced or forgiven loans if students entered scarce professions (Friedman and Friedman 1979). Such plans have been advocated by Canadian economists as well (Rosenbluth and Scott 1985).

A New Canadian Strategy for Funding Higher Education

Wise persons have already given considerable thought to the guiding principles which might underlie any new funding strategy for Canadian higher education:

- encourage universities to raise tuition fees without incurring an offsetting reduction in provincial government grants;
- put more money into the existing Canada Student Loans Program;
- encourage greater variety among institutions;
- give federal support for post-secondary education to the students, and not to provincial governments or institutions;
- adopt an income-contingent loan program;
- provide higher grants to universities which are research-intensive;
- freeze federal government contributions to the provinces.

These proposals of the MacDonald Royal Commission stand the test of both good common sense and time (MacDonald 1985).

The authors would add to this their own conviction that competition among institutions of higher learning is superior to state-sponsored monopoly. Such competition discourages complacency and encourages excellence at the very top. It is also the authors' belief that there are sound economic growth reasons for Canadian public policy to: (a) encourage Canadian institutions of higher learning (of all types) to expand their enrolment further (we envisage a 30 per cent increase over the next decade); (b) expand their budgets in excess of the growth rate of Gross National Product (we would target 4 to 5 per cent annual rate of increase of 'real' funding from all sources, private and public; (c) increase the per-student intensity of their resources; (d) diversify their sources of funding. The latter point inevitably implies a greater degree of 'privatization' of the funding of Canadian universities.

Talk of privatising higher education invokes alarm among that (albeit shrinking) group of academicians who view government officials and politicians as less self-serving and more far-sighted than the rest of the population. For some, a high degree of independence from government would appear to dismantle the very foundation of education. However, we do not share that view.

The authors also believe that more attention should have been paid to the MacDonald Royal Commission when it described the university system as 'a large public-expenditure program in the which the relatively poor groups tend to subsidize the relatively rich' (ibid., p. 747). Social justice requires universities to increase their tuition fees sharply. Income-contingent loans can ensure continued access for lower-income persons.

With these objectives in mind, the authors have simulated various funding regimes. One possible target mix of funding is shown in Table 8. In this approximate 10-year projection, direct government grants to Canadian universities decline from 58 to 25 per cent of the total operating budget, while sponsored research (including a large government-sponsored component as well as joint ventures with industry) rises from 20 to 30 per cent of the total. Tuition fees are approximately doubled as a source of university income, climbing from 12 to 25 per cent of the operating budget and more closely approximating the marginal cost of instruction for these institutions. Gifts from alumni and others also rise, from their meagre 2 to the 5 per cent level—which would still be ungenerous by American standards. Endowment and investment income more than doubles from 4 to 10 per cent of the whole. After a decade, government sources of funding decline to somewhat below 50 per cent, and the fiscal burden upon governments has significantly diminished.

Our suggested plan contains two radical elements. First, for a full decade endowment grants in lieu of expenditure grants are to be given by governments under the condition that they be used to create endowment pools that are totally reinvested for ten to fifteen years for

Table 8
Targeted Sources of Funding for Canadian Universities

	Estimated Current	Target Year 2000
Per cent of Total Funding		
Direct government grants	58%	25%
Sponsored research, gov't and private	20%	30%
Tuition fees	12%	25%
Gifts: alumni and others	2%	5%
Endowment and investment income	4%	10%
Miscellaneous (food services, etc.)	4%	5%
Total	100%	100%

Sources: Nielsen (1985), Leblanc (1987), Statistics Canada (1983, 1988), estimates by authors.

the accumulation of capital. Under a matching-grants scheme, tax expenditures are made by government to encourage the endowment of university funds by private citizens. In this fashion endowment capital is made to grow until it can more than double its present portion of university finance. Some universities will be more successful than others in this regard, and this will have the desired effect of differentiating the fiscal base of various Canadian institutions.

Second, we assume the aggressive conversion of the present Canada Student Loans Program into an income-contingent programme. We estimate the annual rate of lending would rise from its present range of $300 million annually to in excess of $4 billion after a decade. The annual costs of debt service to graduates would approximately quadruple from present levels, assuming a writeoff of about one-half of the loans for income-contingent reasons. In this respect, there will be an on-going major financing role for the federal government, which is projected as eventually writing off as much as three-quarters billion dollars per year. Federal government funding will be redirected, to a significant degree, into student hands, allowing for the exercise of consumer sovereignty in the allocation of higher education dollars, much akin to the admired World War II Veteran's funding programme. Such an initiative would also be an opportunity for the federal government to side-step gracefully the constitutional issues and general muddle that surrounds existing Established Program Funding and freeze, if not phase out contributions to the provinces.

Conclusions

As the OECD study *Universities Under Scrutiny* (1987) has pointed out, two of the dominant international themes relating to universities are first, that the public and governments everywhere are looking to universities, through their education and research functions, to strengthen the competitive edge of their economies; and second, that there has been new emphasis upon the need for improvements in the quality of both inputs to teaching and to research, which implies more resources.

In recent years the public has imposed a third demand: increased access to the system. Growing multitudes frankly view higher education as their 'meal ticket' to better jobs and higher pay.

The dilemma of the universities is how to meet all of these demands within a fiscal environment characterised by accelerating costs and dwindling government support. Amidst all of this, the liberal philosophy of the university must somehow be preserved.

For better or worse, university funding will become more dependent upon market transactions. In the process, the dominance of government will be diminished. This is the universities' opportunity for greater diversification and self-reliance in finance. It is also an opportunity to move more in the direction of quality and diversity in academic programming. These are not necessarily anathematic to the traditions of a liberal institution.

References

Allington, Nigel F.B. 1988. *University Education in Britain: Retrospect and Prospect*, citing the 1985 UK Government WhitePaper, The Development of Higher Education into the 1990s, Canada-UK Colloquium, Institute for Research into Public Policy, Mississauga.

Ardeshir, Noordeh. 1985. *Reforming the Financing Arrangements for Post-Secondary Education in Canada.* Toronto, Ontario: Economic Council.

Bovey, Edmund (Chair). 1984. *Ontario Universities: Options and Futures.* Queen's Printer: The Commission on the Future Development of the Universities of Ontario, December 1984.

Bowen, Ezra, with others. 1986. 'How to Ease the Tuition Load', Time. 4 August 1986, p. 62.

Central Statistical Board of the U.S.S.R. 1986. *The U.S.S.R. in Figures for 1985*. Moscow, Finansy i Statistika Publishers.

Chapman, John W. ed. 1983. *The Western University on Trial.* University of California Press, Berkeley and Los Angeles, California.

Clark, Burton R. 1979. 'The Japanese System of Higher Education in Comparative Perspective'. In Cummings, Ikuo and Kitamura. op. cit.

Corporate-Higher Education Forum. *From Patrons to Partners*. Montreal, p. 80.

Cummings, William K., Amano Ikuo, and Kazuyuki Kitamura. 1979. *Changes in the Japanese University, A Comparative Perspective.* New York: Praeger Publishers.

Davidson, Joe. 1986. 'U.S. Lifting Aid for Students, Mostly as Loans'. *Wall Street Journal.* 29 October 1986, p. 31.

Education Department, United Kingdom Government. 1987. *Annual Abstract and Statistics, No. 123.* 1987 edition. London: Her Majesty's Stationery Office, 1987.

Evangelauf, Jean. 1987. 'Students Borrowing Quintuples in Decade, Raising the Spectre of a Debt Generation'. *The Chronicle of Higher Education.* Vol. 33, No. 17, January 1987, p. 1.

Fisher, James. 1986. 'Funding Education in the Year 2000'. *The New York Times.* 26 November 1986.

Friedman, Milton and Rose Friedman. *Free to Choose.* New York: Avon, pp. 173-175.

Hauptman, M. 1986. 'The Tuition Futures Tax, The Risks Outweigh the Benefits for Families, Colleges and States'. *The Chronicle of Higher Education.* 3 December 1986, p. 96.

Hull, Roger. 1987. 'Preventing a mortgaged future with an Education IRA'. *The Christian Science Monitor.* 4 May 1987, p. 22.

Ichikawa, Shogo. 1979. '*Finance of Higher Education*'. In *Changes in the Japanese University, A Comparative Perspective*, by William K Cummings, Amano Ikuo, and Kazuyuki Kitamura. New York: Praeger Publishers.

Johnson, A.W. 1985. *Giving Greater Point and Purpose to the Federal Financing of Post-Secondary Education in Canada*. Ottawa: Department of Supply and Services.

Kitamura, Kazuyuki. 1979. 'Mass Higher Education'. In Cummings, Ikuo and Kitamura, op. cit.

Leblanc, Hon. Fernand-E. (Chair). 1987. *Federal Policy on Post-Secondary Education*. Ottawa: Minister of Supply and Services Canada, Report of the Standing Senate Committee on National Finance, Second Session, 33rd Parliament of Canada, March 1987.

Leslie, Peter M. 1980. *Canadian Universities, 1980 and Beyond*. AUCC Policy Study No. 3, Ottawa: Association of Universities and Colleges of Canada, September 1980.

MacDonald, J.B. (chair). 1985. *Report of the Royal Commission on the Economic Union and Development Prospects for Canada*. Vol. 2, DSS, Ottawa: (The MacDonald Royal Commission).

Martin, David. 'Trends and Standards in British Higher Education'. In *The Western University on Trial (op. cit.)*, ed. by Chapman.

Maxwell, Judith and Stephanie Currie. 1984. *Partnership for Growth*. Montreal: Corporate Higher Education Forum.

Minister Secretariat, Ministry of Education. 1988. *Japan Statistical Yearbook 1988*. Statistical Bureau, Management Coordination Agency, Tokyo.

Nielsen Task Force. 1985. *Improved Program Delivery: Education & Research*. November 1985.

Nova Scotia. 1985. *Report of the Royal Commission on Post-Secondary Education*. (Rod J. MacLenna, Joan K. Evans, and William S. Shaw, Commissioners), Province of Nova Scotia, Halifax, 18 December 1985.

OECD. 1987. *Universities Under Scrutiny*. Organization for Economic Cooperation and Development, Paris, France.

Rosenbluth, G., and A.D. Scott. 1985. 'The Role of Governments in the Funding of Universities'. *Conference Proceedings*. Toronto: Ontario Economic Council.

Rosovsky, Henry. 1987. 'Highest Education: Our Universities Are the World's Best'. *The New Republic*. 13 & 20 July 1987.

Shils, Edward. 1982. 'Great Britain and the United States: legislators, bureaucrats, and the universities'. In *Universities, Politicians and Bureaucrats, Europe and the United States*, ed. by

Hans Daalder, and Edward Shils. Cambridge: Cambridge University Press.

Shipler, David K. 1984. *Russia*. New York: Penguin Books.

Statistics Canada. 1983. *A Statistical Portrait of Canadian Higher Education*. Ottawa: May 1983.

Statistics Canada. 1988. *Education in Canada 1987*. Ottawa: Canadian Government Publishing Centre.

Tomoda, Yasumasa, and Takekazu Ehara. 1979. 'The Organization and Administration of Individual Universities'. op. cit., Cummings, Ikuo and Kitamura.

UNESCO. 1980 and 1988. *Yearbook of Education Statistics*. Imprimerie Berger Leurault. Nancy, France.

US Department of Education. 1988. Digest of Educational Statistics 1988. Washington: USGPO.

Vobejda, Barbara. 1986. 'Bennet Urges End to U.S. Subsidies on Many Student Loans'. *Washington Post*. 20 November 1986, p. A4.

Watts, Ronald L. 1983. *The Future of the Universities*. Transactions of the Royal Society of Canada. Series IV, Vol. SSI.

Watts, Ronald L. (Chairman). 1987. *New Zealand's Universities, Partners in National Development*. Report of the Universities Review Committee to the New Zealand Vice Chancellor's Committee October 1987, ed. by Dr. Ginette Sullivan. Wellington, New Zealand: Review Committee.

Williams, Dennis A., et. al. 1985. 'Is College Worth It?'. *Newsweek*. 29 April 1985, p. 67.

Wilson, Robin. 1987. 'U.S. Picks 10 Colleges for Loan Plan Tying Repayment to Income'. *The Chronicle of Higher Education*. 20 May 1987, p. 22.

Policies for Access and Expansion in British Higher Education*

JOHN BARNES, LECTURER IN GOVERNMENT
  LONDON SCHOOL OF ECONOMICS AND POLITICAL SCIENCE
NICHOLAS BARR, SENIOR LECTURER IN ECONOMICS
  LONDON SCHOOL OF ECONOMICS AND POLITICAL SCIENCE

This paper sets out policies for the short and medium term to improve access to and allow expansion of higher education in Britain. Currently only 14 per cent of young people proceed to higher education, the lowest figure of any developed economy; and the student population is disproportionately middle class. On both counts, there is room for considerable improvement. Given the move towards a knowledge-based and increasingly competitive international economy, and the need for economic growth to offset the costs of an ageing population, such improvement is vital.

Section 1 sets out some of the deficiencies of the present organisation of British higher education. Sections 2 and 3 establish the building blocks for reform, and section 4 shows how they can be put together into different policy packages.

Problems With the Present British System

The present system has two overriding flaws: it is too centrally planned; and it is too small. The failure of central planning in Britain

---

* This paper draws on earlier work (Barnes and Barr, 1988). Professor Mervyn King suggested the idea of using the National Insurance mechanism for collecting repayments; and Iain Crawford has discussed these ideas with us at every step along the way.

occurs because it is not only restrictive of university autonomy but fails by its own test: it is not conducive to efficiency or effectiveness. In earlier work (Barnes and Barr, 1988), we sketched out the organisational and economic theory which suggests that this outcome is entirely predictable. These arguments need not be repeated here. What does need repetition is the poor quality of the information on which decisions have to be based, the enormous difficulties in its interpretation, the power that this gives to those who have to translate it into a form on which decisions can be based, and the likelihood that such 'uncertainty absorption' will lead to the material being shaped by value judgments, although the outcome will be defended in terms of rational, objective criteria.

Two recent examples illustrate the problems with the present system. First, the recent science review by the University Grants Committee[1] (UGC) determined that no department with fewer than twenty staff was geared to do acceptable research. Six departments with an above-average research record are therefore proposed for closure, two of which have been much more successful in obtaining outside research funding than some of the departments due to be retained. In addition, it is now clear that the Government's desire to raise the number of engineering students by increasing the number of engineering places has had perverse results in that those places have been filled mainly by overseas students, few of whom will continue to work in Britain.

Restricting the Size of the Higher Education Sector

The Treasury has a direct interest in preventing any substantial growth in the number of students in higher education since both tuition fees and the student maintenance grant are funded out of general tax revenues. Even though the grant is means tested on parental income, the Treasury has reduced its real value by a fifth since 1979, and has increasingly brought parents into the parental contribution net (the assessed parental contribution for a typical student is currently about 40 per cent of the full grant). It has also sought to hold down the number of places. Finally, by halving university fee levels in 1981 it made institutions still more dependent on their recurrent grant.

Faced with reductions in funding, the two sides of the 'binary divide'[2] went their separate ways. The UGC, determined to maintain 'the unit of resource' (i.e., real funding per student), held down numbers in universities and threatened to penalise institutions which broke ranks (Kogan and Kogan, 1982). The polytechnics, in contrast, generally took more students, at the price of deteriorating staff-student ratios and reducing their other costs. The government found it convenient to praise the polytechnics for their flexibility. Many of the former teacher-training colleges, however, faced with closure because of falling pupil numbers in schools, took the opportunity to offer higher-education courses of a less-specialised kind, and the government clearly decided that market forces could be taken too far. Anticipating that the decline would work itself through to higher education (whilst forgetting that family numbers were holding up quite well among the middle classes, and largely ignoring the need to increase the participation rate in higher education) it decided to constitute a National Advisory Body (NAB) to rationalise and reduce the number of public-sector institutions.

To the government's consternation the NAB also began to talk about the 'unit of resource'. This should not have been a surprise: it is difficult to see how else meaningful negotiations with the Treasury about funding could take place. The new Funding Councils established by the 1988 Education Reform Act to replace the UGC and NAB have yet to meet, but it is already clear that the Polytechnics and Colleges Funding Council will allocate resources on the basis of student numbers in particular programme areas at particular institutions. The UGC has made no decisions; its Chairman has indicated publicly that he favours moving towards charging economic fees, almost certainly with students borrowing to pay a substantial part, while his principal officer envisages a continuation of the UGC's existing practice. Comment seems superfluous.

However, the unresolved debate has the virtue of drawing to the public's attention the problems inherent in the present system. The government wishes to increase access to higher education. Since they are responsible for funding the relatively low fees charged by higher-education institutions, supplementing them with large recurrent grants via the UGC and financing also the greater part of student maintenance, it is difficult to see how the desire of the Department of Education and Science (DES) to increase access can be accommodated by the Treasury unless and until a loan system is put into place. Anything else will be prohibitively expensive in public expenditure terms, and not likely to be a priority given the increasing demands of an ageing population. Even then, as we suggest below, if the wrong scheme is chosen, Treasury officials may still resist any great expansion for fear that it would add to their growing problems with public expenditure in the medium term.

At present the UGC controls both the price a university may charge and the number of home students it can take, and it is difficult not to see this as a direct consequence of the Treasury's pressure on the DES to keep expenditure down. Indeed, that is precisely what the documents leaked from Conservative policy discussions at Chevening House show.[3] The Under Secretary of State for Higher Education recently said that 19 per cent of qualified applicants to higher education are turned away. This number is not necessarily pinpoint accurate; but its crude magnitude is a considerable indictment of current priorities.[4] Britain is going to be very short of graduates in the 1990s; and the proportion of young people proceeding to higher education is lamentable. Even the most optimistic of present Government scenarios will take the proportion to just under 20 per cent by the year 2000.

Funding Teaching Via Students

Is there a better way forward? It is worth noting immediately two facts: that the money provided to institutions already reflects the numbers they teach; and that students already make choices between institutions. Building on these foundations, we suggest that the funding of teaching and of what may broadly be called scholarship should be met by raising university fees to economic levels, those fees being largely offset by government bursaries to students. The effect of a switch to bursaries would be to channel funds for tuition via the student rather than by recurrent grant directly to the institution.

Research Funding

Before developing this suggestion, we should admit to a problem over the funding of research. There is a strong case for diverse sources and for competition between institutions for a good deal of research funding. Many research contracts will come directly from industry and government departments, and there will also be competition for funds from the Research Councils.[5]

However, it is well-known that immediate utility has proved a very insecure guide to longer-term benefits from research; nor have the established leaders of the various disciplines had a wholly successful track record in spotting profitable research opportunities. Higher education therefore needs to strengthen its endowments, and the government should facilitate this endeavour through pump priming or pound-for-pound payments. It should also continue to provide at least some recurrent funding for departments with a continuing record of successful research and publication. It will not be easy to establish performance indicators to guide the distribution of recurrent funding, but *ex post facto* scrutiny may well suggest which departments have a proven track record.

Attempts to separate research and teaching are ill-judged. Where an institution is engaged in both, it is not possible to do more than arbitrarily to split overhead costs, use of laboratories etc. Higher education fees should therefore include some provision for basic research even though they cannot, in general, bear the full weight. Differentiation should be encouraged not by peer judgment nor by administrative judgments of Solomon, but by a market mechanism which leads postgraduate students to indicate where they can obtain the best sources of guidance, and which will provide some incentive to institutions to specialise in first-degree work.

The Proposed System

It should be stressed that what we propose is a system and not a set of particular proposals. It is possible for governments of different political persuasions to shape the system in accordance with their preferences, and it can be used in a more or less directive manner as the needs of the times or the relative success of particular approaches suggest. There will be no need for any radical changes to the system once it is in place. It is sufficiently flexible to accommodate radical differences of approach, and this is one of its great strengths.

The essence of our proposal is that higher education institutions should be left to conduct their affairs as they wish. They would obtain most of their income directly from those to whom they offer their services of teaching and research. Subject to some safeguards (see below), they would determine their own structure, contractual arrangements with teachers, the courses offered, their nature and duration, their charges for research and eventually their own fee structure. The crucial differences between this system and the present one lie, first, in the absence of government control—but not, as we shall see, government influence—and second in the provision of government support through consumer subsidies rather than the production subsidies characteristic of the present system.

The Influence of Government and Other Actors

Though the proposed system is market-oriented, it does not preclude government action to deal with market failures of various kinds. Indeed, if a government felt able to predict manpower needs in the public sector with some certainty, or manpower needs more generally, this system provides it with incentive-based tools to do a more effective job than it has achieved through the creation of extra places, which are not necessarily filled by home students. For instance, government could offer larger bursaries tied to particular subjects. In addition, with the loan system discussed below, forgiveness of part or all of a loan in proportion to the number of years engaged in a particular type of job is a powerful tool for influencing individual decisions.

A major advantage of the strategy is the plurality of influences it allows to shape the system of higher education, not just the institutions but other sponsors of students, and the students themselves. Manpower planning has always proved an uncertain science; the market is a classic way for others to hedge the government's bets. Many firms already provide bursaries, and there are also public-sector institutions who finance their students through college. The London School of Economics, for example, has mature students from the police college at Bramshill. We envisage that government departments other than the DES might wish to provide bursaries for specific purposes just as they already commission research, an outcome which is good in itself, not least because it makes decision-taking more transparent.

Students as Consumers

Whether or not it is advantageous to give more power to students as consumers depends crucially on how well they are equipped to make choices. Critics of their ability to do so need to be reminded that unless we are to move to direction of labour, students already make choices and that (judged in terms of their private rate of return) their ability to turn those choices to profit looks rather better than the judgments of manpower planners. The latter ignore the highly pragmatic reasons which underlie industry's refusal to assess their manpower needs too far into the future, and firms' preference for recruiting students with good honours degrees whatever the subject. Planners tend to have a more narrowly vocational view of the subject matter of courses than those who recruit for industry, and seem ready to ignore uncomfortable truths: not only is there very little graduate unemployment, but humanities subjects like history and philosophy clearly have their vocational side. Accountancy firms do not recruit those with first qualifications in accounting in preference to all other degrees, and information technology has identified a considerable need for philosophy graduates.

The present position indicates that potential students or their surrogates can and do make choices, but the information on which they act clearly needs strengthening. Our confidence in their ability to operate in a market-oriented system should not be mistaken for complacency about the existing state of careers advice, nor any belief that competent use is always made of careers conventions or the existing guides to institutional provision. In general, less is known by students about the polytechnics than the universities, and less still about colleges of higher education. It is an essential part of our proposals that much more information should be published and that there should be an 'office of fair trading' to guard against misrepresentation.

Advantages

Of the many advantages, three stand out. First, higher education will be responsive to the demand of various actors: students, their employers and government. Second, institutions will have a real incentive to teach well. Currently, universities have both the home fee level and home student numbers effectively dictated to them. Their home fee income is thus pre-determined. It is scarcely surprising, therefore, that teaching plays little part in promotion, and that academics have every incentive to concentrate on research. Nor have higher-education institutions had much incentive to develop shorter courses or modular courses which can be combined with other activities.

A third major advantage is that institutions would be dependent on attracting students to survive, and would therefore be responsive, innovative and flexible. They would also be more cost conscious, and would no longer have to devote time and money to finding ways of bending a centralised planning system to their advantage. They are likely to become more differentiated as a result, but the form of that differentiation will almost certainly reflect society's needs more accurately than the rather rigid categorisation inevitable in any bureaucratic decision. The rigid distinction drawn in Britain between further education and higher education seems peculiarly indefensible.[6]

Safeguards

Implicit in all we have said is the need not only for better information, but for satisfactory measures to assure quality. In Britain, the Council for National Academic Awards (CNAA) has developed effective ways of assessing courses at polytechnics, and more recently has turned its attention to the appropriate institutional mechanisms to ensure that these standards are maintained between periodic reviews. Even if their expertise is not used directly, it can inform the search for satisfactory means of quality assurance. The activities of Her Majesty's Inspectorate, who publish reviews of particular institutions, offer an alternative. Our preference would be for publication rather than administrative regulation as the prime sanction: with schools, publication of inspection reports has sharpened the performance of institutions. In the last resort, however, the government could decide that state bursaries would no longer be tenable on a particular course or at a particular institution.

Looked at in reverse, such a mechanism affords a way for a newly established private sector institution to move into a position where it could attract some state funding on particular courses. This would lessen the present very high hurdles which have deterred all new institutions from entering higher education apart from the University of Buckingham.

Loans

Bursaries offer only one part of the way forward. It is crucial to an expanding system of higher education that there should be a properly organised loan scheme. We welcome both the government's commitment to loans and the almost universal recognition in the press that this was the right route forward. Less welcome was the particular form of many of the government's White Paper proposals (United Kingdom, 1988), and the inability of the existing student body to recognise that this is a three-way debate, i.e., between grants, mortgage-type loans (which are organised like a mortgage of bank loan), and loans with income-related repayments.

The Debate About Loans

The proponents of grants naturally set up mortgage-type loans as their target, but many of their criticisms are dealt with automatically in an income-related scheme of the type set out below; in addition, that scheme, unlike either the present system or the White Paper proposals, would be conducive to greater access.

Perhaps it is natural for a privileged class to protect its privileges, but students in Britain need to recognise the wrong-headedness of their claim that any system other than outright grants will deter students from disadvantaged backgrounds from entering higher education. The evidence shows that the existing system, expensive though it is in terms of public subsidy, brings into higher education less than seven per cent of the relevant age group with a working class background. It has been well characterised as a 'middle class rip-off'. It draws its students disproportionately from the best-off, and it takes the great majority through to well paid occupations where they earn much more than the bulk of taxpayers who finance the student through college.

Still more to the point, grants are a very expensive way of financing students and this encourages the Treasury to resist expansion. It is no accident that we have an expensive system of student support and a small higher-education system. Almost every other country resorts to loans or some combination of loan and grant to ensure that they have a substantially larger proportion of the population going into higher education. Proud though we are of the Open University and now the Open College, they are no substitute for an expanded higher-education system.

Criticism of the White Paper (United Kingdom, 1988)

If we are fully behind the government's case for loans, we are critical of the particular scheme adopted. It is worth stressing, however, the extent to which the government has left the detail of the scheme open to debate, an outcome which is to be welcomed. We propose a number of constructive alternatives and will criticise the White Paper largely by implication. However, it is worth making some direct criticisms. First, the finance comes entirely from government, but the decision to involve the banks in running the scheme will throw large costs on to them and also makes a government guarantee essential to allow for the 10 per cent default rate (i.e., fraudulent non-repayment) plus the 15 per cent rate of write-off (i.e., where students do not earn enough to repay in full) assumed in the White Paper. It is therefore an expensive scheme which does not become self-financing in the course of the next decade and a half, and the Treasury is unlikely to want to extend it. Thus it does nothing for access.

A further cost element arises because the loan, though indexed, has a zero interest rate. Thus there is a 2-3 per cent interest subsidy, and a substantial incentive to every student to take the maximum amount, and to reinvest the proceeds at a profit.

Finally, unless repayments are income-related and made over an extended period, the deterrent effects feared by representative student bodies (and the authors) will be justified. Students, particularly from poorer backgrounds, unused to the thought of going into higher education and ill-informed about its likely benefits, are going to set the possibility of heavy debt against the advantages of immediate income. They do this already at 16 and need to be encouraged to continue into the sixth form and beyond.[7] The way to do so is to use the public-sector resources saved by loans (a) to create more places in higher education, (b) for policies to prevent students dropping out at age 16, and (c) to offer students from disadvantaged backgrounds a larger maintenance grant or, in the longer term, a larger bursary.

A Loan Proposal

The best way to avoid any deterrence is to create a repayment scheme which is equitable and which relates repayments to a student's subsequent earnings. Thresholds below which repayment is suspended reduce the problem of the low-paid, but at the expense of an acute poverty trap or, if there are a series of thresholds, a series of poverty traps. Such a poverty trap is all the more a problem if the government wishes to encourage married women graduates to rejoin the labour force. Better a more smoothly graduated scheme. However, the most obvious candidate, a graduate tax, is already facing difficulties in Australia, not least because of the difficulty in defining the income to be taxed. Taxes are in any case a standing incentive to evasion. They are not likely to be seen as the fairest way in which to repay a loan. What we propose for Britain is a scheme based on National Insurance Contributions (NICs), which will operate only until the individual loan and the accrued interest is repaid. Repayments would take the form of a small addition to the contribution already paid on earnings up to the upper earnings limit established under the NICs.

The scheme has major advantages. Practically everyone pays NICs and accumulates benefits such as the retirement pension. In principle, contributing for a benefit in the future is no different from paying for one already received. The scheme involves borrowing from oneself while earning to pay for benefits when not, and to that extent, it is easily explained and readily defended. Loans for education are no more than an up-front pension. Because other benefits are involved, there is no incentive to evade payment, and unless the student emigrates before making any contribution, there are future benefits or past contributions which could be attached in settlement of outstanding debts.

Using the scheme for this purpose actually strengthens the contributory principle and arguably lessens dependency, something which should be attractive to the present government and not unacceptable to others. Employers too can be required to make a contribution via the employer NIC. At a time when graduates are going to be a scarce commodity, it makes sense for employers to pay a small charge (a maximum of 160 a year for an extra 1p employer contribution) on the graduates they employ. Note that employers thereby contribute only to the education of those graduates whom they choose to employ. The state might remit some or all of these contributions for certain occupations, and it would in any case top up the loan fund in respect of those unable to repay in full. Since students, employers and the state all benefit from higher education, it is efficient to have tripartite sources of funds.

The sums involved over a repayment period of 25 years are very small. It would be possible to replace half the grant by an indexed loan, repayable by an extra NIC of 1 p in the pound shared between the graduate and his/her employer.

There are enormous advantages if the finance to start the scheme comes from the private sector (e.g., the banks and/or employers), with repayments collected through the National Insurance mechanism. Given that the risk of default and write-off is low, there would be no need for any substantial Treasury guarantee. As a result, from the very first, the scheme could be self-financing in public-sector terms, and hence easily extensible. The result would be to enhance access and release resources for expansion (for further discussion, see Barr, 1989). The public-sector savings are so large that they could finance an expansion of student numbers of 20 per cent and perhaps even more.

Policy Packages
Different Policy Mixes

It is possible to introduce loans without bursaries or vice-versa. However, the two combine logically into a complete system of funding for higher education which can be set according to the current preferences of government, but which remains free of their control and open to other influences.

The system can be set at any point along the dimensions shown in stylised form by Figure 1. The horizontal axis shows the spectrum from full central planning at one extreme to a totally free market at the other. The vertical axis moves from redistribution from rich to poor via distributional neutrality to regressive redistribution. The present system is somewhat regressive and highly planned, represented in Figure 1 by the point P.

The possibilities are illustrated in Table 1. In model 1 the state assumes a nightwatchman role in respect both of educational intervention and redistribution, represented stylistically by point 1 in Figure 1. At the other extreme, in model 3 the state is educationally interventionist and the system is strongly redistributive (point 3 in Figure 1). Model 2 is an intermediate case. Different models can be used for different aspects of funding, e.g., interventionist in terms of bursaries, redistributive in terms of maintenance and laissez-faire in terms of fees.

Figure 1
Different Types of Intervention

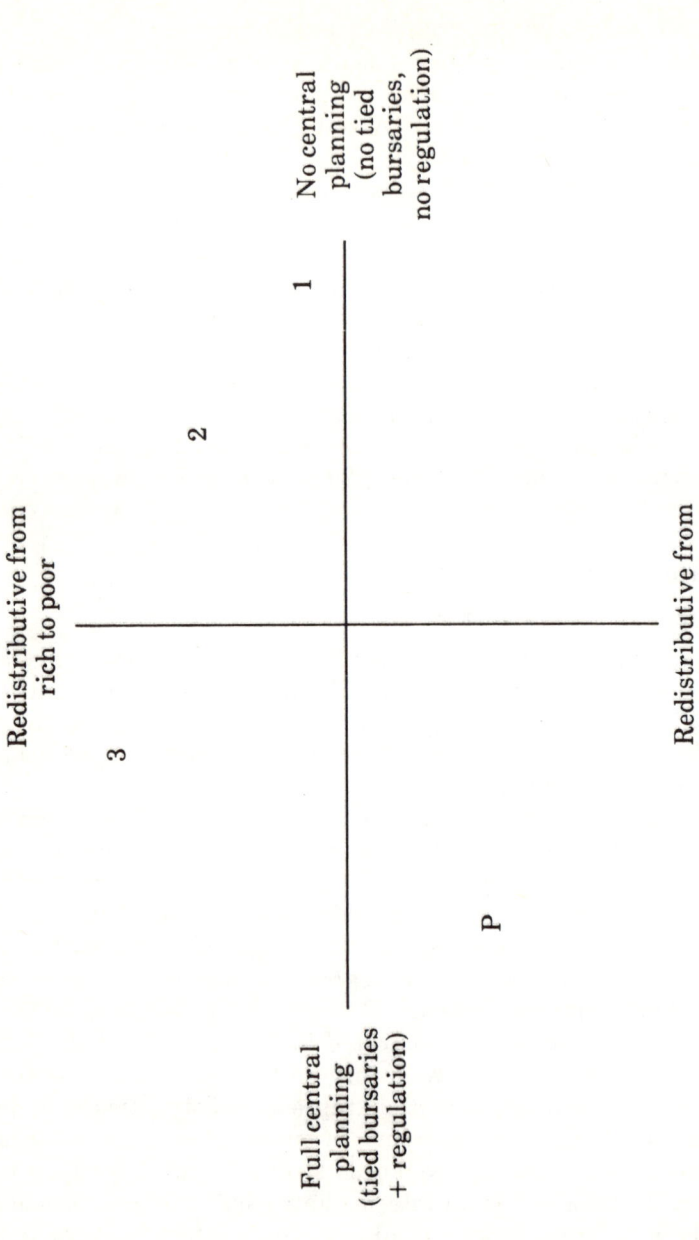

Redistributive from rich to poor

No central planning (no tied bursaries, no regulation)

1

2

3

Full central planning (tied bursaries + regulation)

P

Redistributive from poor to rich

Table 1
Alternative Models of Higher Education

	Model 1: NIGHTWATCHMAN	Model 2: INTERMEDIATE	Model 3: INTERVENTIONIST
FEES	Unconstrained	Unconstrained or flexible within state-ordained limits	Flexible within state-ordained limits or fixed by government

BURSARIES	Level: average tuition fee
	
	Restriction in use: none
		Level: average tuition fee
		    higher for disadvantaged students
		    higher for skill shortages
		
		Restriction in use:
		    protection of some subjects/institutions
			Level: tuition fee + contribution to maintenance
			    fees + full maintenance for disadvantaged students
			
			Restriction in use:
			    extra bursaries tied to subjects the government wishes to encourage
			    tied bursaries to protect some subjects/institutions

MAINTENANCE	Commercial loans with at least partial state guarantee Student's own plus family resources Bursaries from industry Private philanthropy	Income-related loans, repayable till loan paid off Student's own plus family resources Bursaries from industry	Graduate tax, repayable for life for students with bursaries not covering full maintenance Loans could be forgiven/partially abated for students from disadvantaged backgrounds or going into certain subjects Student's own plus family resources
RESEARCH	University endowments Contracts from government Contracts from industry Any surplus on fees	University endowments Residual recurrent grant Specific grants from Research Councils Contracts from government Contracts from industry Any surplus on fees	Continuing recurrent grant Specific grants from Research Councils Contracts from industry Any surplus on fees
REGULATION	Quality: Voluntary (mandatory?) publication of relevant information Director of Fair Trading (?) Quantity: No regulation of student numbers	Quality: Mandatory publication of relevant information Mandatory external examiners Director of Fair Trading Quantity: Maximum number of state bursaries at any one institution (?)	Quality: Mandatory external examiners Quantity: Maximum number of state bursaries at any one institution

Conclusion

All too often the debate in Europe and in much of the Commonwealth about the funding of higher education has tended to polarise around horror stories of nationalisation and complete privatisation. The former works badly because of the asymmetries of information between the organisations involved and the near inevitability of organisation failure. Even were this not the case, however, there are good reasons why universities should be independent of the state, and the longer-term interests of both liberal democracy and the knowledge-based economy are best served by a high degree of autonomy for higher education. That need not force us to the extremes of privatisation and the spectres which British Vice-Chancellors clearly see raised by the recent pronouncements of the newly-appointed Chairman of the UFC (see the interview with Lord Chilver in the *Times Higher Education Supplement*, 14 October 1988, p. 9).

A regulated market offers both competition and co-ordination, and goes a long way towards resolving the difficulties posed for government by the choice between the extremes of nationalisation and privatisation. Its advantages are so enormous that our main surprise has been that the idea has hitherto made so little headway. In Britain the recent experiences of universities at the hands of the UGC, the increased burdens of planning and its self-evident biases and ineffectiveness have led to very serious consideration by Vice-Chancellors and the DES of a regulated market. It has also found considerable support in the serious press and among colleagues. Perhaps its time has come.

Glossary

Bursary: a payment by government (or other institutions) to students to enable them to pay full economic fees. The bursary will generally be equal to or above full economic fees. Under the resulting system the government finances higher education largely by giving money to students rather than to higher education institutions.

CNAA: (Council for National Academic Awards): a watchdog body which polices the quality of degrees offered by polytechnics in England and Wales.

DES: Department of Education and Science.

NICs: (National Insurance Contributions): levied in the United Kingdom on all employees, usually at a rate of 9 pence in the pound on earnings up to the upper earnings limit (305 per week in 1988/89).

PCFC: (Polytechnics and Colleges Funding Council): a new body established by the Education Reform Act 1988, which will fund polytechnics and colleges by offering contracts for the teaching of specified courses or subject areas. See also UFC.

UFC: (Universities Funding Council): a new body established by the Education Reform Act 1988, which will fund universities by offering contracts for the teaching of specified courses or subject areas. See also PCFC.

UGC: (University Grants Committee): a body abolished by the Education Reform Act 1988. Its original function was to fund universities by giving them recurrent grants, but increasingly it found itself drawn into assessing their relative efficiency and rationalising the provision of higher education in the university sector.

Notes

1. The University Grants Committee (UGC) is a buffer between central government and the universities. The government hands over to the UGC each year the great bulk of funding for the university system as a whole. The division of the total among the different universities is a matter for the UGC. Formerly such recurrent grant came with no (or virtually no) strings; latterly, the UGC has been increasingly directive as to the way individual universities should spend UGC funding.

2. The 'binary divide' is a term coined in the sixties to reflect the fact that higher education in Britain is delivered in part by 'private sector' universities and in part by polytechnics and colleges, which were then largely under local authority control. Although they have now achieved independent status under the 1988 Education Reform Act, the polytechnics and higher education colleges have not been assimilated but remain separately funded so far as Government grants are concerned. Public funds are channelled to universities by the newly instituted Universities Funding Council (UFC) and to polytechnics and colleges by the Polytechnics and Colleges Funding Council (PCFC).

3. Chevening House is the official home of the Foreign Secretary, who has spearheaded many Conservative policy reviews and has considerable sympathy for 'voucher' type solutions.

4. The most recent figures suggest that the percentage of those turned away has fallen to single figures as the overall decline in the birth rate between 1965 and 1975 works its way through to the age groups entering higher education.

5. The various Research Councils receive block grants from the central government, which they use to fund individual research projects on the basis of research proposals.

6. Higher education relates to degree courses. Further education is concerned with qualifications beyond minimum school leaving age but below degree level. The worst feature of the distinction is the rigid demarcation between the two sectors.

7. Staying on at school beyond the fifth year of secondary education is voluntary; the same is true of entry into other forms of further education. Some of the resources devoted to improving access should be directed at this stage in the educational process.

References

Barnes, A.J.L., and N.A. Barr. 1988. *Strategies for Higher Education: The Alternative White Paper*. Aberdeen University Press, for the David Hume Institute and the Suntory-Toyota International Centre for Economics and Related Disciplines, London School of Economics and Political Science.

Barr, N.A. 1989. 'Student Loans: The Story So Far and the Way to Go'. *Public Money and Management* (forthcoming).

Kogan, M. and D. Kogan. 1982. The Attack on Higher Education, Kogan Page.

UK (1988). Top-Up Loans for Students. Cm 520. London: HMSO.

III

GOVERNANCE AND ACCOUNTABILITY

The Governance and Funding of University Education in Britain: Retrospect and Prospect

NIGEL F.B. ALLINGTON

UNIVERSITY OF WALES COLLEGE OF CARDIFF

Introduction

The history of university education in recent years has been dominated by the idea of more for less. By the end of 1985 the Department of Education and Science in the United Kingdom was hoping for an annual reduction of 3 per cent in the number of lecturers and looking for staff/student ratios of 9:1.[1] Soon after, a 50,000 rise in student numbers was being predicted for 1990 representing 153,000 additional full and part-time students in higher education over the 1979 levels. But real income of universities has been falling constantly; in 1986 universities were told to expect reductions of about 11 per cent over the following four years. In the preceding financial year they had already received a reduction of 3.5 per cent on grant compared to costs, given that university costs rise about 1.5 per cent more than the rate of inflation.

Universities have responded by cutting back: there have been numerous retirements, closure of departments, a virtual freeze on appointments in many areas, especially the humanities, as well as on short-term contracts. Whole disciplines have been pummelled—the travails of philosophy, for example, are well known.[2] Sadly, the universities have shown none of the imaginative flair and managerial competence that might have softened the impact of retrenchment, though they have shown initiative in recruiting overseas postgraduate students, often at the cost of making a mockery of their traditional academic standards.[3] What we have not seen in any useful measure is computer-generated fundraising efforts targeted at alumni in the professional solicitation of business and the wealthy. Nor have we seen a drive for more efficiency in the work of administrators and secretarial staff, or the substitution of student labour for porters and attendants. Nor has the potential of the campus been fully utilised; much of it is idle during vacations, evenings and weekends, even in strategic locations like London—fittings and so on are too substandard to attract business.

Such creative impoverishment has been more than matched by the inflexibility of the state. Universities' power of decision-making is handcuffed by the bureaucracy. The number of undergraduates they can take is firmly limited.[4] They cannot plan because of uncertainties in the area of funding. There is, in fact, only one policy towards universities; cut their income in the hope that they will generate it privately. Since universities do not at present possess the will to do this, or, alternately, to produce something for which there is a high private demand, their response has been to cut commensurately from the fat down now to the muscle.

In particular, the government has failed to offer universities any alternatives to the drip feed of state funding. Uniquely, the present Conservative government sees no alternative to state monopoly, and universities remain the only area of national life where the state monopoly goes unchallenged even by the most rhinoceros of backbenchers. The government attacks the universities for failing to behave like private bodies, yet refuses to give them the freedom that would allow them to do so because, in the end, it fears any challenge to the notion of merit as the exclusive criteria of entry to higher education. To preserve this principle, it is prepared to blight the future of intellectual life in Britain.

The Shift to Vocational and Technological Relevance

The 1985 *Green Paper, The Development of Higher Education into the 1990's*,[5] must be seen as a depressing document by anyone concerned with the traditional values of education. The humanities merit scarcely a mention; marketability rather than intellectual depth is the criterion.

The *Green Paper* emphasises the need for a better trained technocracy, with more qualified scientists, engineers and technologists, with the emphasis on vocational courses if Britain is to remain internationally competitive. Higher education is diagnosed as being in need of adopting a less snobbish attitude towards industry and commerce. The essentiality of the entrepreneurial spirit, the need to foster positive attitudes to work, the need for students to be able to work co-operatively in groups, are all stressed. It reiterates just about every tired cliché that might have once been heard in the boardroom.

Thus the *Green Paper* reveals in its pronouncements an image of universities as merely an ante-chamber to the commercial world and the purpose of learning as the development of the economy rather than the development of the individual. Such a view is not new; it is the attitude against which John Newman rebelled in the nineteenth century with the *Idea of a University*.[6] It is a view impregnated with a utilitarianism that would see no use for history, literature or any branch of learning that did not have commercial significance. In this it is strictly contemporary with the homage to relevance, that infatuation with the current, which mark our instant gratification culture.

It is to be doubted too whether the things demanded by the *Green Paper* can be inculcated pedagogically, for they are culturally transmitted. In prescribing so fully what the values of universities ought to be, the *Green Paper* betrays a dangerous authoritarianism which should further alarm those who see little good in the state monopoly of university education.

Access to Higher Education

With some justice the *Green Paper* emphasises the importance of increasing access to higher education, partly to satisfy the demand of business for graduates in the nineteen nineties. The participation rate amongst the relevant 18/19 cohort is expected to increase from 14 per cent to 18.5 per cent or even 20 per cent by the year 2000.[7] The need to include students with a wider set of practical and academic experience, stressing the importance of admitting students with vocational qualifications and the necessity of rethinking teaching methods receives attention. However no deleterious effects are perceived to follow from this change. But, in the movement from an elite culture to an instrument of mass society, standards are bound to suffer. We must have the intellectual honesty to admit that more students will mean something worse, or if not, different for universities. Also we must accept that integrity of standards cannot be the exclusive consideration even if it must rank high. The needs of commerce for highly trained personnel must be recognized as well as the matter of whether more people could benefit from higher education in terms of leading richer and more fulfilled lives. The question is, could standards be stretched sufficiently to accommodate them without ceasing to exist meaningfully? It is to be regretted too that the *Green Paper* does not advocate the more demanding alternative; namely, the improvement of secondary education, so that a dilution of university standards is not necessary. The *Education Reform Law* deals with this satisfactorily up to the age of 16, but the all-important 16-18 education provision has been wilfully neglected and the *Higginson Report* apparently shelved.[8]

University Funding

On the question of funding, the *Green Paper* points out that the typical British university receives over 90 per cent of its income from government funds, funnelled largely through the University Grants Committee (UGC), soon to be replaced by the University Funding Council (UFC). Money also comes from fees, largely via Local Education Authorities, who receive a 90 per cent grant from the exchequer. Research Councils, also publicly funded, contribute something. In addition to the full cost of their tuition, British students also receive a means-tested maintenance grant. Table 1 gives the main sources of income in British universities under these headings for three comparative academic years.

The *Green Paper* is sceptical about such a system and points to the alternative methods of student support in other countries, particularly the American National Defence Student Loan Programme.[9] However, it concludes that no substantial part of established public funding responsibilities can be shed. Rather cynically it is prepared to conserve a public monopoly even though it is run badly, in obeisance to some dogma which says that universities must be public to preserve standards. A broader concept of standards might include such things as the simple continuity of scholarships in now-threatened areas. By denying the privatisation option and the freedom it would bring, the State is guaranteeing the complete running-down of the British university system.

Selectivity Exercises

The *Green Paper* also argues for the concentration of research expenditures, thereby implying selectivity, and does not find a compelling reason for all academic staff to engage in research. Whole universities as well as whole departments would lose research funding through the UGC. This strikes at the very essence of a university and what distinguishes it from a training factory. Subtract research and you cease to have a university. A university is, moreover, a corporate entity; to eliminate research in one department is to change the over-

Table 1
Main Sources of Income in British Universities 1970-1986

	1970/71	1980/81	1986/87
Exchequer (UGC Block) Grants	71.2%	62.6%	55.0%
Fees	6.3	17.2	13.7
Research Grants & Contracts	12.7	12.9	19.4
Income from other Services	2.9	2.9	6.1
Endowments & Gifts etc.	1.5	0.9	1.3
Other Recurrent Income	5.3	3.7	4.5
Recurrent Income (Mn) = 100%			
(Current Prices)	316	1,563	2,484
(1980 Prices)	1,374	1,563	1,749
Non Recurrent Exchequer Grants			
(Current Prices)	68	104	143
(1980 Prices)	296	104	101
TOTAL INCOME			
(Current Prices)	384	1,667	2,627
(1980 Prices)	1,670	1,667	1,850
Student Loan	237,069	311,985	313,416
Recurrent Income per Student (1980 Prices)			
Exchequer (UGC Block) Grant	4,118	3,136	3,072
Fees	367	862	764
Other	1,302	1,012	1,746
TOTAL	5,787	5,010	5,581

Source: University Statistics, Volume 3, "Finance", 1987.

all climate and detract from the research potential of all. Many areas of research, especially in the arts and social sciences, need little in the way of expensive equipment, so that to grade them non-research is vindictive. Selectivity means that large players attempt to monopolise resources by devaluing the input of smaller players. The claim that smaller departments are inefficient and therefore disposable merits considerable intellectual scepticism. A research reputation helps to attract students nationally and internationally students like to receive knowledge from those who are actively adding to it.

Selectivity implies judgement, but the indices chosen are particularly clumsy and embody fallacious reasoning. Student performance after graduation is preferred and the *Jarratt Report*'s suggestions for performance indicators within and among universities are welcomed.[10] Student performance is measured on a short-term basis, thereby favouring those with applied qualifications, whereas the *Jarratt Report* approach is mechanical and clearly requires interpretative and qualitative judgement to avoid a highly distorted picture.

Much emphasis is placed on the relevance of research and the possibility of its commercial and industrial exploitation. It is extraordinary that the State should feel it can prescribe and redefine academic values so precisely; this is comprehensible only in the light of its monopoly position. Those who favour intellectual liberty must wish this to change. Extraordinary too is the locus of the blame; universities are seen as the errant party in their relationship with industry, never once is business castigated for shortsightedness in failing to draw talent from universities, or to help supplement their income. The behaviour of that which is private must be right, even though as Correlli Barnett so memorably demonstrated in The *Audit of War*,[11] the pragmatic bias of British industrialists has often given them a mindless contempt for abstracted and theoretic reasoning and a consequent impoverishment of their competitive effectiveness.

The Management of the System

The UGC continues to stress the importance of rationalising small departments, even advising on minimum size. The *Oxburgh Report* of 1987,[12] a review of earth sciences, was the UGC's first attempt to rationalise a science and was the harbinger of more to come. It advocated the closure of small departments and the concentration of research in 10 or 12 centres of international standing. Level 2 would offer up to Master's degree level and not receive costly equipment; Level 3 would merely do first- or second-level undergraduate teaching and probably not maintain separate science departments. The UGC has reported recently on chemistry and physics departments and concludes that only a few can be supported for top research.

The notion of concentrating money in top institutions has much to recommend it: the criticism surely is that in these parsimonious times, it is seen as achievable only at the cost of depriving other universities of their departments, or downgrading them into pedagogic academies. The menace of this argument is that it does not conceive of a university as an organism whose components reinforce each other by drawing its life from its variety; rather it is seen as a mechanical feeder into some vast, abstract research machine. Therefore the closure of a department diminishes the vitality of the entire institution and makes it ever less than the classical conception of a university. Downgrading a department to teaching status deprives students of the excitement of a direct connection to the frontiers of knowledge. The moribundity of such departments would be unimaginable and their ability to attract students doubtful.

The Advisory Board for the Research Councils (ABRC) promulgated a three-tier strategy for Britain's science base: Type R would be teaching and research; Type T would be undergraduate teaching and Masters work, with low-level research facilities, and Type X would be primarily teaching, with research only in particular fields.[13] The ABRC argues that whole institutions should be designated, not just individual departments. It also echoed the *Oxburgh Report* in claiming that, on the basis of the American experience, large centres were the most effective performers in areas of research. But, as one commentator has pointed out, the vogue for universities developing specialisations contains the risk of everyone choosing the same fashionable areas of expansion—information technology, materials science, biochemistry and biophysics.

The proposals neglect the contribution the smaller departments make to the total community: the difficulties posed by assessment and the tendency to promote the *status quo*; the dangers of creating inflexible and unimaginative monoliths instead of great research centres; the ability of smaller departments to foster individualism and the problem of inducing creative thought in large, highly managed institutions. Whilst none of this is an argument against creating great research centres, it is an argument against denuding the whole system to do so.

Ranking Exercises

If universities and departments are to be ranked according to the quality of their research, a mechanism has to be found for so doing. The academic consensus is that productivity is the best guide to research activity and that referred publications in reputable journals are the most direct index of productivity. However, by introducing a heavy reliance on conspicuous expenditure and on personal judgements of the worth of particular types of research, the UGC has substituted a complicated and hidden process.

It is not surprising, therefore, that the various rankings produced in 1986 were hotly disputed.[14] In Electronics and Electrical Engineering, for example, the UGC had rated Imperial College only as 'above average'; a peer review by heads of department rated it second. Glasgow, starred by the UGC, was average in the peer review. There were enough similar instances to induce the Institute of Chemical Engineers to produce its own criteria for evaluating research. Table 2 gives the results of the UGC ranking exercise for 1986 in summary form, together with the *Times Higher Educational Supplement* peer review and a hybrid rank combining the two. A second UGC review of research was started in late 1988 and promises much greater sophistication, but this remains to be seen.[15]

A particular source of concern in the first exercise was the use of research income in the evaluations. Income from industrial sources seems, ironically, to have been ignored by the UGC but given greater weight by the Research Councils. Yet, a low level of research income does not necessarily mean a low level or quality of research in the humanities.

While evaluation exercises invariably are flawed, they should still be attempted, for they reduce complacency, encourage self-criticism and create a climate of competition rather than co-existence. But their limitations must be clearly understood; qualitative and impressionistic factors should be written down, as well as mathematical weightings, otherwise the process becomes mechanical. Therefore, their usage in allocating resources, as distinct from simply providing feedback, must be circumscribed by a process of discussion and consultation.

After the UGC evaluations, the ABRC enumerated its current criteria for evaluating research; in general, external factors were to be given a heightened role. The criteria for evaluating scientific priorities are thus: timeliness, the expectation of quick results (between 5 and 20 years); persuasiveness, (the connection with other research); commercial exploitability; as well as social and other benefits.

If these criteria are to be applied, any serious defender of intellectual liberty must be alarmed. It is important that scientific research should feed into economic growth, but which line will eventually do this is a difficult matter to judge. Also, scientists wish to extend their knowledge of man, matter, and the universe, to dive to the

Table 2
University Grants Committee Rankings

Social Sciences and Humanities	All Subjects Combined	Natural Sciences, Engineering and Technology
1. Bristol	1. Cambridge	1. Cambridge
2. Manchester	2. Manchester	2. UCL
3. Edinburgh	3. Edinburgh	3. Oxford
4. Leeds	4. Bristol	4. Edinburgh
5. Cambridge	5. UCL	5. Manchester
6. Nottingham	6. Oxford	6. Liverpool
7. Glasgow	7. Leeds	7. Imperial
8. UCL	8. Glasgow	8. Bristol
9. Oxford	9. Nottingham	9. Leeds
10. Durham	10. Newcastle	10. Newcastle
11. Warwick	11. Liverpool	11. Glasgow
12. Reading	12. Southampton	12. UMIST
13. Lancaster	13. Sheffield	13. Cardiff
14. East Anglia	14. Birmingham	14. Southampton
15. Southampton	15. Warwick	15. Bradford

Table 2a
Times Higher Educational Supplement Peer Review

Social Sciences and Humanities	All Subjects Combined	Natural Sciences and Engineering
1. Oxford	1. Cambridge	1. Imperial
2. Cambridge	2. Oxford	2. Cambridge
3. UCL	3. Imperial	3. Oxford
4. Manchester	4. Edinburgh	4. Edinburgh
5. Warwick	5. UCL	5. Bristol
6. Edinburgh	6. Manchester	6. Birmingham
7. Bristol	7. Bristol	7. Leeds
8. Leeds	8. Leeds	8. Manchester
9. Sussex	9. Warwick	9. UMIST
10. St. Andrews	10. Birmingham	10. UCL
11. Essex	11. Sheffield	11. Glasgow
12. Exeter	12. Sussex	12. Sheffield
13. Lancaster	13. UMIST	13. Southampton
14. York	14. Newcastle	14. Sussex
15. Sheffield	15. York	15. Newcastle

Table 2b
Poll of Pools

Research Universities	Mixed Universities	Teaching Universities
1. Cambridge	16. Kings College London	36. Heriot-Watt
2. Oxford	17. UMIST	37. Aston
3. Edinburgh	18. Liverpool	38. Kent
4. University College London	19. Strathclyde	39. Exeter
5. Manchester	20. Sussex	40. Swansea
6. Bristol	21. Cardiff	41. Hull
7. Imperial College London	22. Leicester	42. Brunel
8. Leeds	23. York	43. Aberystwyth
9. Birmingham	24. Lancaster	44. Bangor
10. Glasgow	25. Loughborough	45. Bradford
11. Southampton	26. East Anglia	46. Salford
12. Newcastle	27. Reading	47. Stirling
13. Nottingham	28. Durham	
14. Sheffield	29. Dundee	
15. Warwick	30. Aberdeen	
	31. Bath	
	32. Essex	
	33. Surrey	
	34. Queens' University Belfast	
	35. St. Andrews	

causes of things and disinter the wellspring of being. To subordinate this noble aspiration to the nagging demand for relevance is to bondage the soul of scientific curiosity.

The state, in its relationship with universities, is increasingly seeking the role of investor to consumer. It demands clear and quantifiable returns and this would be the trend whatever party was in power. Such a trend is inimical to the spirit of intellectual curiosity, an emotion which those who advocate it presumably have never experienced.

Therefore, it is not only the libertarian thinker who might dream of severing the links that tie universities to the state, but academics who might otherwise applaud a welfare state ought to judge with increasing scepticism the British state's total monopoly of their institutions as well.

Meeting the Challenge—A Tripartite System of Funding in the Future

The central recommendation of this paper is independence for several universities under an endowment scheme equivalent to ten years of a recurrent grant, that would ultimately generate 100 per cent of the present recurrent or block grant. The endowment would be subscribed to by government and industry, possibly on the basis of equal contributions. A survey of a number of top British firms has confirmed that there is significant support for such a scheme and the result would be that the state becomes a junior partner in university funding.[16] Although this represents a significant outlay, its confinement to a few institutions each year would not stretch Treasury resources unduly. The state would also offer support to students through a flexible voucher scheme that would cover a portion of the cost of degree courses and maintenance—the number and value of the vouchers would be determined by government to reflect national needs and priorities. Universities would set their own full-cost fees to cover tuition and maintenance. At least 20 to 25 per cent of these total costs, together with the difference between the voucher and the fees, would be retrieved through a graduate tax. This would be paid through enhanced income tax, where graduate earnings are at, or above, average earnings.[17] Where this is not the case—for example, through unemployment or low earnings, or confinement in the case of women—repayment would be waived. The endowment fund and vouchers, plus any additional costs to be met temporarily by the state that arise from the difference between full-cost fees and the voucher, together with benefactions and alumni donations, which make up any short-fall in total income, would create entirely independent and self-governing institutions. The candidate institutions must have a period of preparation in order to organise for the change-over, and industry would need to be given details of the endowment schemes in order to decide whether they feel able to offer support in each particular case.

The benefits would be considerable. With complete autonomy of decision making accorded to universities, including the ability to pay high salaries and attract big names, these institutions would be free to attract larger numbers of students on a full-fee basis. The state's commitment would now be the up-front voucher costs. The United States has some very good private universities, including some of the most famous, and there is no reason why this could not be done in Britain. Parents would no longer be expected to meet their share of the means-tested maintenance grant and students would be directly responsible for meeting a portion of the costs of their own education. This would create a greater awareness of the costs as well as the benefits of a university education, something at the present time that is mainly taken for granted.

Moreover, attractive universities could build up substantial conference or short-course income during vacations. They could create summer programmes with foreign universities. There is undoubtedly a large market for evening university education in the region, and by correspondence elsewhere that is presently monopolised by the Open University. Like most American universities, students themselves could perform many of the functions done by ancillary staff, thus offsetting part of their personal costs.

There is no reason to believe that universities would not be enterprising; any hostility to such ideas by the universities would be evidence of the peculiar rigidity which marks all thinking on higher education in establishment circles. Ministers believe that endowments would make academics lazy—one quoting Gibbon's description of eighteenth-century Oxford. There is no evidence to show that academics at Harvard, Yale or Princeton are lazy. Indeed academic inertia—a problem with universities all over the world—is more likely to descend on the pensioners of the state. Independence would create a dynamic that would invigorate all limbs of the institution.

Proactive Policy in the Interim—Administration

Whilst some universities remain temporarily in the public sector, government strategy, which has been a negative one of incremental cost-cutting, should become more thoughtful and also more proactive. Many of the issues discussed in the following paragraphs will be equally pertinent to the private university too. The aim will be efficiency and a desire to awaken intellectual morale, as well as to revive the moribund state of many disciplines: to make universities feel they are worthwhile and to give them a sense of hope and awareness that industry, achievement and style will be properly rewarded.

The analysis must begin at the top. The vigour of the corporation derives in part from the personality and competence of the chief officer. Vice-chancellors often do not perform as well as expected. The central criticisms are: ignorance of funding and marketing techniques; limited ability to communicate; the use of cost-cutting rather than proactive initiatives; bureaucratic administrative style; inability to switch from research to corporate leadership—in Britain at present over 50 per cent of vice-chancellors are former academic scientists. The mediocrity of leadership has harmed the universities and requires redress. This includes the introduction of five-year contracts; more appointments from industry and commerce to improve management;

periods of training at a staff college to inculcate skills of personnel management, fundraising, marketing, public relations and the like.

Within the administration arm of universities there is an urgent need for the importation of new skills and new agencies. Every university requires an alumni office with its requisite skills. The more progressive universities like St. Andrews (under the tutelage of an American vice-chancellor) have already adopted this approach and several others are belatedly entering the field. A marketing office is required to attract candidates and promote the facilities and services of the campus to industry and commerce both at home and overseas. More emphasis needs to be placed on encouraging American and European students to read one year at a British university. Generally, administrators should be selected from outside higher education in order to broaden the skills available. Here the staff training college will be important in initiating and retraining administrators. The administrative structures of universities must be streamlined too, for their organisation is extremely clumsy, leading to delay and inflexibility.

Aspects of a National Strategy

Universities are hampered in their ability to deal with their crises by factors beyond their control, which are state manufactured. This is particularly true in the planning process where the government's financial commitment is paramount. The government has explicitly rejected the *Croham Report*'s advocacy of triennial funding,[18] which can analyse existing trends and resources and assess likely cash flows over at least four years.

To make universities efficient, the government must give them the minimum sums they are likely to receive over a five-year period. Next, universities must be given external support targets and create a strategy for achieving an average of 25 per cent private funding—smaller for liberal arts, higher for technological universities. Vice-chancellors and senior staff must be held accountable and their activities must be subject to investigation.

A royal commission on higher education to investigate the state and future of British universities is also recommended. The protracted period of crisis makes this important. Moreover, the many ideas that have been put forward for the improvement of both quality and efficiency of the system need more thorough investigation by a dispassionate enquiry. The imagination that Robbins brought to his report must be the quality of any commission's work.[19] It would signify that government took universities seriously and recognised that all was not well.

The research councils, which occupy a strategic role, especially in scientific, engineering and social research, are also in urgent need of reform. In particular, they should supply a full critique when an application for funding has been rejected; this would give useful feedback. Next, they must act speedily so that researchers can turn to alternative sources of funding; re-submission should also be allowed. Academic personnel should change regularly so that no individual school of thought or professional network gains a monopoly of ideas. The research councils should seek some element of private support for their work; several have expressed a desire to do this in the future.

Next, the creation of a national brokerage agency to mediate between universities and industry is essential. Its task would be to market research-to-client businesses and communicate relevant feedback to university departments. This organisation would be started in conjunction with the private sector, with a view to its eventual privatisation.[20]

Students—Participation and Education

Graduates are the principal product of a university and the education they receive gives them a career that literally is enriched, since they can expect to double what their salary might have been without a degree. The state pays dearly for this. In addition to the grant, it costs about £17,500 to produce an arts graduate, double that for a scientist and even more for a medic. For its part the community receives dividends in taxes and in other ways for the investment made by the state.

Nevertheless, if the state wishes to raise participation rates, ways must be found to lower the costs. Universities can be made more efficient. However, some costs can be recouped by offering students a lower level of service or by making them or their subsequent employers pay more for the privilege.

In Britain, university education costs include boarding, and the concomitant costs to the exchequer are high.[21] Thus, a move towards more student participation might draw initially on local candidates. Technical and vocational degrees should extract more of a monetary subsidy from students and their future employers because they are more expensive. The teaching staff could be of poor quality—the best people are lured into commerce—yet their students are highly employable because what they are doing is as much training as education. Law, management, engineering and some of the applied sciences would all carry such a cost, for whilst the state has a moral duty to subsidise the intellectual development of the individual, it does not have a similar commitment to the training programmes of industry, commerce and the professions. At the moment, state resources are building up vocational departments at the expense of the humanities.

Therefore, graduates (perhaps with the assistance of their employers) whose income is at or above average earnings should pay enhanced income taxes to meet something more than 20 to 25 per cent of tuition and maintenance costs for these courses. The state could make exceptions in areas where there are skill shortages and offer compensation to students choosing subjects considered to be under threat. There is, of course, a serious problem of equity; would those from poorer backgrounds be actively dissuaded from going to university if the price becomes too high, thereby undermining its *raison d'etre* as an agent of social mobility? Surely this is a patronising attitude— because they have not been put off mortgages—and the pursuit of equity has consigned academic life to mediocrity. Firms might also pay a recruitment fee to universities where they are not contributors to endowment funds. This would represent a substantial source of new income. Again, the precise logistics of the scheme should be left to the proposed royal commission.

Currently, there is wide discussion of a voucher/bursary system of student funding.[22] This would allow competition and a freer market amongst universities; popular departments or institutions could expand and students would have more choice. Students would have a clearer idea of the value of their degree schemes. Universities would be much more concerned with providing an effective service to students. The danger with this scenario is that vocational subjects might drive out other disciplines. When a subject and its intellectual tradition has been lost it cannot easily be resurrected. The government would have to distribute vouchers to guard against this, although the industry survey referred to above indicates a high demand for arts and social science graduates—generalists rather than inventors and innovators.

There seems to be no compelling reason for retaining the University Central Council for Admissions (UCCA). Universities in the United States do not rig the market in this way, nor do they suffer from not having a bureaucratic central admissions system. UCCA represents an artificial restriction on freedom of choice, hampers competition between universities and leads to the absurdity of rejecting students if they do not put a university high on the list.

The state also should cease to fund student unions, and membership should be made non-compulsory; the taxpayer does not subsidise the discotheques in town, why should he subsidise on-campus entertainment?

There is the highly contentious issue of the content of the subjects taught. The humanities and social sciences are both menaced by the pressure of relevance and of contemporaneity. Sadly, the problem with a consumer approach to university education is that it will magnify these pressures. It is legitimate to fear how far commitment to teaching, what Gertrude Himmelfarb described as 'the best there is', will be completely eroded.[23] To defend the best there is, each discipline should have its own review body monitoring content and standards, not acting as an obtrusive intellectual policeman nor conserving a mummified corpse, but alerting the public if the integrity of disciplines is consistently violated. If universities cease to transmit high culture, there is absolutely no point in public funding of any sort. Universities should be free to teach the widest range of subjects, but government should not be under an obligation to fund them; let them generate their income from private industry and students.

Some element of student assessment needs to be built in to degree schemes: their main merit would be to guide lecturers; their use as a mode of evaluating academics is somewhat dubious.[24] However, without such an instrument there is no incentive over and above conscience and professional elan, for academics to develop as effective teachers. That said, clearly teaching ability is not as important as it is in schools, since students are self-motivated and can acquire information independently. However, it is important that they should feel affection for the subject and that is something poor teaching can kill.

Academic Personnel

Substantial changes in the incentive and career structure of academics are needed in British universities. The present structure represents an attempt to transfer the Oxbridge conception of cloistered livelihood to a mass profession and to repeat on a large scale the prerequisites of an elite order. The central problems are: the academic profession is inert in non-vocational areas—soon the average age of university lecturers will be 48; pay scales range for a lecturer from £9,400 to £20,000 by increments irrespective of performance; through tenure, academics are inviolate and mediocrity cannot be replaced; promotions are blocked mainly through financing problems; and all academics are expected to achieve equally at teaching, administration and research, although these are separate competencies.

The structure of the profession therefore is in need of reform to reward the able and motivate the more lethargic. This is better done by positive incentives rather than negative sanctions.

Tenure should be modified rather than abolished, conforming to the American model, where it is given as a reward not a right and often after a period of perhaps eight years or so. This would have the added advantage of preserving academic mobility internationally. The abolition of tenure might lead to great political purges. No other profession would tolerate such conditions and, indeed, in many areas of commercial life there is some form of tenure. In fact, the government has abolished tenure for all promotions and all new appointments under the 1988 *Education Reform Act*;[25] thus the most able and mobile are penalised, which is precisely the opposite effect of what a thoughtful reward system would achieve. The modification of tenure means that academic freedom needs to be enshrined in legislation; academics simply cannot be trusted to observe intellectual tolerance. Such is their emotional commitment that, as well as vigorous defenders, they can be able persecutors. Advances often come from challenging orthodoxy, yet those in power often owe their position to perpetuating that orthodoxy, so that fresh thinking is perceived as a threat.

Next, academics should specialise in research, teaching or administration. Researchers and administrators would continue to teach, but carry a lighter load. Individuals would elect initially which track to be placed in: later they would be judged on how well they had justified their election, so that research does not become a way of avoiding chores. Certainly it is absurd that professors who obtain the rank through skill should have to spend most of their time on administration. This is a misdirection of resources that marks the entire system.

More contentiously, academics should be paid much more, with an average increase of 25 per cent to compensate for salary erosion. Even higher rates should be offered in fields that are difficult to recruit in, with geographic differences in pay to reflect local labour market conditions.[26] These increases will be possible in view of the alternative methods of funding discussed before. The end result would be the invigoration of morale and the recruitment of highly qualified candidates. At the present time many of the most able enter commerce, finding the vow of poverty intolerable. Moreover, a salary increase would have important symbolic effects, demonstrating that the government had tired of the philistine caricature and was determined to re-awaken academic life through diversified funding.

There is the additional problem of the entry blockage to the academic profession. The problem is posed by taking most academics from one generation and then repeating the cycle when they retire. Again, the opportunities afforded by diversified funding can help to relieve this situation and coincidentally revive the great traditional disciplines of the humanities, classics, history, philosophy, literature, languages, geography and political science. Much more needs to be done for the sciences than the new-blood schemes were able to achieve.

Tax Funding and Concluding Remarks

Recent developments, such as the taxing of gifts to endow chairs, suggest that a wider review of the tax system is necessary. This should aim at encouraging tax-free donations as state subsidies decline. In the United States, institutions benefit strongly from such a system and it has the merit of directing revenue to favoured areas without the bureaucratic mediation of the state.

The general principle of funding adopted here is one that would best serve institutions and their consumers with the latter, the direct beneficiaries, paying something more than the normal taxpayer for services which materially advance them. It must be accepted that the arts and social sciences may suffer under this system, but that every effort should be made to invigorate them with assistance from the taxpayer and industry, if only through a graduate tax. Any notion of contract funding is rejected and great importance must be placed on the preservation of university independence. To give Whitehall total control, which is the clear implication of the *Education Reform Act*, would subordinate universities to the particular economic and social politics that were the flavour of the moment.[27] Some latitude must be preserved; it is for example unfortunate that the cuts of 1981 were uniformly imposed with no judgement being exercised over which subjects were most meritorious in particular universities.

Universities' policy represents one way for government to emerge as firm accountants, but committed to the defence of cultural values, for it is culture more than technology that defines a civilisation. Academic excellence and academic freedom have proved incompatible with state control of the universities. Independence by degrees offers the chance to escape from intellectual bondage. In Professor E.H. Carr's words, 'it is significant that the nationalisation of thought has proceeded everywhere pari passu with the nationalisation of industry'.[28] Nowhere is that more evident than in the universities. Perhaps it is now time to denationalise thought.

Notes

1. M. Kogan and D. Kogan, The Attack on Higher Education, London, 1983, p. 11.

2. Philosophy has been undermined seriously in Britain so that there are at present only 57 full-time philosophers under the age of 40 in the country. However, student demand is buoyant and employment prospects good, with high demand in the fields of information technology and computer programming. Rather belatedly the University Grants Committee is now calling for eight chairs to be filled in the subject, for selected universities although no new finance is available to make these appointments.

3. The decision to charge full-cost fees to overseas students from September 1980 resulted in a fall in enrolments as expected, but by academic year 1982-83, the decline had been arrested. A clear pattern of differentiated fees is emerging now as individual universities set their own fees in the area. With increasing competition from overseas institutions, however, the transitory nature of this lucrative source of income is well understood, and marketing of courses is becoming more aggressive. Cf. J. Sizer, 'Institutional Responses to Financial Reductions in the University Sector', *Department of Education and Science Research Project,* Paper 3, 1986, pp.17-18.

4. Until 1987 undergraduate entry was determined quite rigidly by the University Grants Committee with stiff penalties for exceeding them, but universities can now accept more students, although no extra resources beyond tuition and maintenance fees will be made available.

5. *The Development of Higher Education into the 1990's,* London, HMSO, Cmnd. 9524, 1985.

6. John Henry Newman, *The Idea of a University,* New York, 1959.

7. Kenneth Baker, Secretary of State for Education and Science, Lancaster Speech, 'Higher Education: The Next 25 Years', University of Lancaster, January, 1989.

8. 'Advancing A Levels', *Report of Committee Appointed by the Secretary of State for Education and Secretary of State for Wales,* (The Higginson Report), London, HMSO, 1988.

9. OECD, 'Country Study; The United States of America', *Changing Patterns of Finance in Higher Education,* 1989.

10. *Report of the Steering Committee for Efficiency Studies in Universities,* (The Jarratt Report), Committee of Vice Chancellors and Principals, 1984.

11. Correlli Barnett, *The Audit of War; The Illusion and Reality of Britain as a Great Nation*, MacMillan, 1988.

12. *Strengthening University Earth Sciences*, (The Oxburgh Report), University Grants Committee, 1987.

13. *A Strategy for the Science Base*, The Advisory Board for the Research Councils, 1987.

14. University Grants Committee, 'Planning for the Late 1980's', Circular Letter 12/85, 1985.

15. University Grants Committee, 'Research Selectivity Exercise', Circular Letter 45/88, 1988.

16. N.F.B. Allington and N.J. O'Shaughnessy, 'Teachers and Traders: A Survey of Industry Attitudes to Universities and Funding', *Oxford Journal of Education*, forthcoming 1989.

17. Full analysis of the scheme can be found in: N.F.B. Allington and N.J. O'Shaughnessy, *The Future of British University Education*, The Fulmer Press for The Institute of Economic Affairs, London, forthcoming 1989.

18. *Review of the University Grants Committee*, (The Croham Report), London, HMSO, Cmnd. 81, 1987.

19. *Higher Education: Report of the Committee Appointed by the Prime Minister Under the Chairmanship of Lord Robbins*, (The Robbins Report), London, HMSO, Cmnd. 2154, 1963.

20. The difficulty industry experiences in establishing contact with universities to commission research emerged in the industry survey, 'Teachers and Traders: A Survey of Industry Attitudes to Universities and Funding', *op. cit.*

21. See Table 1.

22. A.J.L. Barnes and N.A. Barr, *Strategies for Higher Education: The Alternative White Paper*, Aberdeen University Press for the David Hume Institute, London School of Economics, 1988. Cf. N.A. Barr, 'Student Loans: The Next Step', London School of Economics, 1988.

23. Gertrude Himmelfarb, *New History and Old*, Boston, 1987.

24. Student assessment of lecturers is to be part of the lecturer appraisal procedure agreed between the CVCP and the lecturers

union The Association of University Teachers (AUT), starting in the academic year 1989-90.

25. *The Education Reform Act 1988*, London, HMSO, 1988.

26. There are early signs that national pay bargaining will be broken, as St. Andrews reaches agreement on an independent increase, with specific employment conditions attached. The University of Wales College of Cardiff looks as if it will be the second so to do.

27. J. Griffith, 'The Threat to Higher Education', *The Political Quarterly*, 1989. Cf. N.F.B. Allington and N.J. O'Shaughnessy, 'The Threat to Universities and Proactive Responses, A Reply to Griffith', *The Political Quarterly*, forthcoming 1989.

28. E.H. Carr, *What is History*, London, 1986, p. 48.

Accountability and Autonomy in Canada's University Sector: Business as Usual or the Lull Before the Storm?*

J. CUTT, PROFESSOR, SCHOOL OF PUBLIC ADMINISTRATION
UNIVERSITY OF VICTORIA
ROD DOBELL, PRESIDENT
THE INSTITUTE FOR RESEARCH ON PUBLIC POLICY

Introduction: Scholars under Scrutiny

The possible entry of legislative auditors into the assessment of performance of academic institutions has recently become a matter of colourful debate (in a few restricted circles) in Canada. Possible movements of governments towards contracting for prescribed 'outputs' from post-secondary institutions have generated cries of alarm. The threat of exposure of academic institutions to the chill winds of competition with commercial suppliers of education services has shaken some university quarters. Controversies over alleged underfunding of universities, transition to direct funding of students, unwarranted government intrusion in the determination of academic priorities, the threats to academic freedom inherent in government direction of academe, have all raged for some time. The questions of autonomy in academic life, independence in scholarship, discretion in research are obviously crucial, and there seems little doubt that some of the actions presently under consideration could seriously weaken the independence of existing post-secondary institutions in Canada. So the issue is important.

---

* This note is drawn from a larger monograph being prepared by J. Cutt in association with A.R. Dobell in the Victoria office of the Institute for Research on Public Policy.

The thesis of this note, however, is simple: greater accountability can assure continued autonomy and contribute to improved funding prospects. In brief, the taxpayer deserves a better explanation than currently offered of what universities accomplish with the resources made available, and why some departures from competitive market mechanisms in the allocation and management of those resources may be useful. Institutions which live off annual allocations cannot afford the luxury of insisting on being taken on faith at all times.

Unfortunately, to develop a persuasive argument that this simple thesis is also plausible and defensible demands a rather extensive tour through some background on funding mechanisms and reporting requirements. In Canada, given federal-provincial jurisdictional issues, the story is particularly turgid. The importance of the debate warrants the effort, however, remote as the material may sometimes seem.

A Digression on Mechanisms for Control or Accountability

The university sector in Canada expanded dramatically in the 1960s and early 1970s, becoming in the course of this expansion essentially a ward of the state. In this period governments which paid for the expansion of institutions and programmes generally appeared to accept the view, held by universities, that peer and professional control coupled with the control exercised by boards of governors provided a sufficient framework of indirect control. In their view, government direct control should be limited to prior approval of university budgets in the aggregate, (either for individual institutions, or, where an intermediary body had been established, for the university sector as a whole), to occasional short-term earmarking of funds for new programmes and to auditing of the financial statements prepared by universities. The question of value for money was raised only in terms of whether enough was being spent to meet the expanding needs asserted by universities. Funders took the 'value' provided by this money as self-evident; in short, the question was not posed, either with respect to controls on decision-making autonomy by universities or on accountability for such decisions. As in the United Kingdom, however, by the late 1970s the relationship between government and the universities had changed. More difficult economic times required more careful choice in the use of scarce resources and, in the absence of persuasive evidence of the value provided by the funds allocated to universities, governments turned to a more detailed framework of direct control. This framework of control is summarized below and is detailed more fully in the annex to this paper.

Governments can employ two sets of instruments for controlling universities. The first set is directed at limiting the decision-making autonomy of universities, while the second attempts to increase university accountability.

In limiting decision-making autonomy, governments may draw on a wide variety of instruments. These range from controlling the membership of boards of governors of universities to requiring, before funding, detailed information on planning and budgeting. This might even go so far as to require explicit statements about management systems, controls, and practices.

After providing the money, governments may insist on increased accountability that goes beyond straight financial accounting and legislative compliance. This could even reach the point where management is being asked to make representations on value for money; in other words, economy, efficiency and effectiveness.

Up to now, budget (funding) levels have provided the most obvious government instrument for control of university activity, and this instrument is obviously of direct concern to both sides.

Mechanisms such as earmarking of funds or contracting for services are also important direct influences, while retrospective reporting or value-for-money audit requirements may be seen as more of a nuisance than a direct constraint on university decision-making.

The point of this paper, however, is that by addressing this latter instrument in an enlightened and responsive manner, universities may be able to ease the threat of more vigorous exercise of the former, and much less palatable, instrument.

The approach to the balance of this note will be to deal briefly with the two levels of government involved, the federal and provincial, and then, for each level of government, to sketch the traditional pattern of control, the evolving pattern of increased direct control, and the response of universities. The argument seeks to demonstrate the gap between what governments are moving towards and what universities appear willing to provide. The identification of the gap is intended to provide universities with an opportunity to take control of the agenda of change by developing and providing the requisite information on value for money, in considerable part by drawing on information presently prepared for management purposes internally, but not reported externally.

The Players

In Canada, education is constitutionally a provincial responsibility, and it is therefore at the provincial level that the foundations of the control framework, both in terms of structure and information prescriptions and requirements, are to be found. Nevertheless a major feature of the evolving framework of control in Canada has been the increasing frustration of the federal government, which has come to foot the larger share of the bill, with the absence of any influence on— or indeed, any mechanism establishing accountability for use of the funds provided under the existing fiscal arrangements. The federal role and the variety of recent recommendations for change in that role are therefore considered as a context for consideration of approaches by provincial governments.

Figure I shows the major players in post-secondary education financing in Canada, the flows of funds (solid lines), and the accountability relationships (dotted lines). The relationship between provincial governments and the universities is clear. Provincial governments provide operating grants (amounting to between 75 and 80 per cent of university funding) either directly or through an intermediary agency, and universities are correspondingly accountable; the actual flow of accountability information falls far short of that increasingly sought by provincial governments and legislative auditors. This gap will be a primary concern later in this note; for the moment, it is the role of the federal government which is of particular interest.

The larger part of the funds which eventually reach universities as operating and capital grants comes from the federal government in the form of transfers to the provincial governments. These transfers are made under the Established Programmes Financing Act of 1977, are unconditional in nature, and require no formal accountability in reporting. The federal government, through its granting agencies, also provides 60 per cent of direct research funds to faculty members in universities, and receives direct project-specific accountability reports on these grants. This granting does, however, require universities to bear the indirect or overhead costs of research, an issue to be discussed below under Established Programmes Financing (EPF) funding.

The Perspective of the Federal Government

The federal government has contributed to post-secondary education in a variety of indirect ways in Canada, starting soon after Confederation. The modern era of federal support for post-secondary education dates, however, from 1951 when Ottawa, in response to a recommendation of the Massey Commission, began a programme of direct grants to universities to help defray operating costs. Since then, federal policy for supporting post-secondary education can be classified in three phases: direct grants to universities from 1951 to 1967; cost-sharing with the provinces of all post-secondary education from 1967

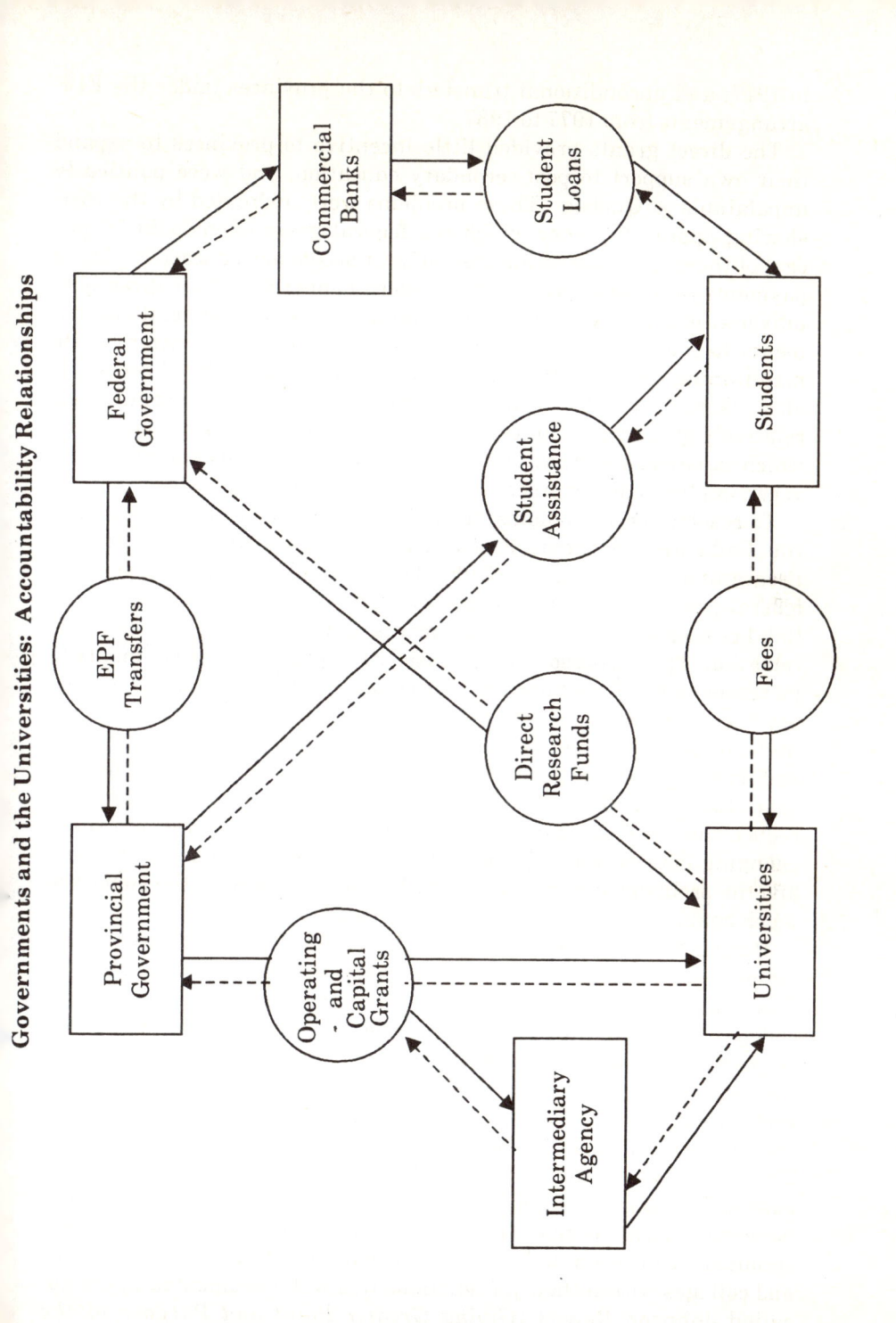

Governments and the Universities: Accountability Relationships

to 1977; and unconditional transfers to the provinces under the EPF arrangements from 1977 to 1987.

The direct grants provided little incentive to provinces to expand their own support to post-secondary education, and were politically unpalatable to Quebec. These problems were addressed by the cost-sharing approach, under which the federal government paid 50 per cent of the eligible operating costs of post-secondary education. These payments were made to provincial governments rather than directly to universities. This system provided an incentive to provincial governments to increase expenditures on post-secondary education while maintaining their constitutional jurisdiction in the area. However, it also resulted in a loss of federal control over its own expenditures, relatively greater per capita payment to the so-called 'have' provinces which expanded their post-secondary systems relatively rapidly, and a very complex auditing process for determining eligible costs.

To resolve these problems, the federal government, in 1977, passed the Federal-Provincial Fiscal Arrangements and Established Programmes Financing Act (EPF). Under this Act, which still governs federal-provincial transfers in respect of post-secondary education, the link between federal transfer payments and post-secondary costs was removed. This Act also tied increases in federal transfer payments to increases in GNP, and provided for equal per capita payments to each province. Actual transfers to provinces have been affected by the fact that part of the transfer is in cash and part is in 'tax points', by the 'six and five' programme that resulted in a reduction in transfers for the years 1983 to 1985, and by the 1986 amendment to the Act designed to reduce the net federal transfer by 2 per cent by 1991. Despite these changing details, the principles established in 1977 have remained, and the problems inherent in the EPF system have been the subject of much heat and a little light for the last decade.

During the second phase of the period (1967-1977) of federal support for post-secondary education, both major levels of government in Canada accepted responsibility as partners in funding Canada's colleges and universities. The provinces retained their constitutional responsibility, but the federal government's support for 50 per cent of the operating costs of post-secondary education gave implicit recognition to the concept of a national interest or purpose. With EPF the nature of this political partnership changed in a fundamental way. The incentive to the provinces to contribute to post-secondary education was greatly diminished, and the change in the relationship between federal contributions to the provinces in respect of post-secondary education and actual provincial grants to the universities and colleges within their jurisdictions was well documented in the so-called Johnson Report (*Giving Greater Point and Purpose to the*

Federal Financing of Post-Secondary Education and Research in Canada, a report prepared for the Secretary of State of Canada, February 15, 1985). This report argues that the federal share of the total costs of post-secondary education had risen and the provincial share had fallen to the point where, in five provinces, federal transfer payments in respect of post-secondary education actually exceeded the total amount of provincial grants to post-secondary institutions. In effect, the report implies that the partnership between the two levels of government in support of post-secondary education had been replaced in these provinces by a system of federal funding, and in the other provinces, that the 1977 balance had been seriously eroded.

The provinces, faced with tougher economic times and other pressing priorities, had responded by cutting back sharply on spending on post-secondary education, and the most immediate result of the change in the federal system for support for post-secondary education in 1977 was thus a significant decrease, relative to the growth in GNP, in the support of the core operations of universities and colleges. In the decade after 1977, enrolment in universities increased sharply concurrently with the reduction in relative funding, and the real income per student in post-secondary institutions has therefore dropped significantly—by approximately 30 per cent—since the introduction of EPF.

It should be stressed that the provinces have not contravened any formal agreements or regulations. It is clear that the EPF Act was intended to provide them with precisely this freedom and flexibility. But provincial responses to those guaranteed, unconditional federal transfers has created a climate of frustration and mistrust and a commitment to finding ways of changing the system. The issue has been visited in a series of reports. The Parliamentary Task Force on Federal-Provincial Fiscal Arrangements in 1981 recommended the formal separation of EPF transfers for health and post-secondary education, and this division was made in 1984. No changes were suggested by the Parliamentary Task Force, however, in the block-grant system of funding, and the frustration of the federal government manifested itself more clearly in later reports. The Johnson report in 1985 recommended that the growth of EPF payments should be harmonized with provincial operating grants by increasing EPF payments at the then rate of increase (geared to GNP and population) only if provinces did likewise. Johnson went on to reject other options: using the cash portion of EPF funding for universal student grants or vouchers, or for a massive increase in research funding, and the withdrawal of federal support for the core operations of universities. The 1985 Macdonald Commission report was also strongly critical of the current EPF funding arrangement and went on to recommend the consideration of a range of options including replacing a portion of existing EPF cash transfers with voucher payments to students, freezing current federal cash contributions and tying future contributions to matching provincial expenditures, and using some of the funds released by freezing the federal contributions to fund university research.

The Nielson Task Force Education and Research Study Team report in 1986 also reviewed EPF payments critically, and considered but did not decide among various options: making future federal support conditional on agreement by the provinces to meet specified standards; the provision of federal funds to students directly through some such system as vouchers; and the recognition by the federal government that it had no role in post-secondary education and should therefore withdraw its financial support completely. In March 1987, the Standing Senate Committee on National Finance also considered the matter carefully and recommended that the federal government terminate the post-secondary portion of EPF payments and deal with the matter by transferring adequate financial resources through tax points to provincial government.

The general question of the federal role in funding remains uncertain. Most recently, at the National Forum on Post-Secondary Education in Saskatoon, Saskatchewan in October 1987, there was broad agreement on the need for a continuing partnership of the federal and provincial governments in addressing post-secondary education, but also an unwillingness on the part of the federal government to increase its contributions without some role in determining how the money should be spent and some accountability for that spending.

If little agreement has emerged on the general federal role in funding other, than perhaps, the need for a change, there would appear to be increasing agreement that federal funding of sponsored research should be increased to include the indirect costs of such research. The present system imposes these indirect costs on university operating budgets, and, in a period of straitened budgets, has had what are generally agreed to be deleterious effects on university research. This issue has been addressed in various reports, including a strong recommendation by the Standing Senate Committee on National Finance that the budgets of the granting councils be extended to cover these indirect costs. More ominously, however, the Macdonald Commission report and the Johnson report noted that increased federal funding for sponsored research would probably have to be financed at least partly at the expense of general core funding through EPF grants. Core funding, of course, is intended to cover all operating activities in universities, including research. The diversion of federal support from core funding grants to sponsored research would represent essentially the functional earmarking of a larger portion of federal contributions to post-secondary education in a manner not dissimilar to that currently practised by the University Grants Committee in its calculations of grants to universities in the United Kingdom.

Currently federal contributions are equivalent to 80 per cent of university operating grants in Canada. While federal withdrawal seems unlikely, the erosion of the level of these contributions in a variety of directions does seem likely. Given scarce federal resources, it is possible that there could be a replacement of part of the general core funding by more comprehensive grants in the area of sponsored research, including both direct and indirect costs. Some universities would, of course, applaud increases in sponsored research funding, but may have disregarded the implications for what, in effect, will become increased functional earmarking, diminished autonomy in resource allocation decision-making, and sharply increased direct accountability for research funding.

The influence of the federal government has also extended to other policy instruments and targets, particularly to the recurrent theme of establishing national objectives in post-secondary education. The Parliamentary Task Force in 1981 suggested that

> early attention should be given to the definition of purposes in post-secondary education that are of concern to all governments. In this connection, we would see priority consideration being given to the need for more highly qualified manpower in the 1980s and the confirmation of existing commitments to student mobility and equality of access to post-secondary education of Canadians (p. 130).

In 1982, the Minister of Finance indicated that the federal government expected to see a shift in the priorities in post-secondary objectives in favour of manpower training, failing which he would consider freezing EPF transfers for post-secondary education. The Johnson report in 1985 reiterated the importance and appropriateness of national objectives including such objectives as accessibility for all qualified students in Canada, high quality education and related research, improvement in the employment potential of students of all ages, the right to student mobility across the country, and the right of taxpayers to a full accounting of the sources of finance for post-secondary education (Giving Greater Point and Purpose to the Federal Financing of Post-Secondary Education and Research in Canada, pp. 33-34).

There is, of course, less difficulty with the concept of national objectives in principle than there is in practice. Agreement on the importance of a national agenda or mandate for post-secondary education appears to be growing. It emerged as perhaps the primary theme of the National Forum on Post-Secondary Education in Saskatoon in October 1987. The evolution of such a set of objectives and perhaps also an acceptable mechanism for their implementation, such as through the Council of Ministers of Education, Canada, now seems likely. More specifically, the objectives of quality (or excellence) and accessibility recur in the debate over the federal role in the last decade. The Johnson report paid particular attention to the development of 'world-class centres of excellence' and the theme was reiterated by the recent report of the Standing Senate Committee on National Finance. In this specific sense, excellence is taken to mean excellence in research, and the implications for federal funding appear to go beyond the specification of objectives to the concentration of funding or institutional earmarking in order to achieve this objective. Accessibility is another common theme. Ironically, this objective was reiterated by the Johnson report, but also criticized by Johnson as the exclusive preoccupation of university funding at the expense of excellence! The question of accessibility was, however, a major preoccupation of the National Forum and it seems likely that the trade-off between excellence and accessibility will be a theme in any reform of the federal role in financing post-secondary education in Canada.

Related to accessibility is the larger question of who benefits and who loses. Only the Macdonald Commission has been vulgar enough to accept fully the argument of Friedman, Weisbrod, and others that spending by the federal government on post-secondary education is counter-redistributive in nature, and to translate this concern into recommendations for higher student loans and voucher-financing (although Wright Commission proposals in Ontario in the early 1970s for contingent repayment schemes for student assistance went a long way in this direction). This question does not appear to be at the highest level of priority in current federal thinking about post-secondary education, but bears consideration as a complement to the larger question of accessibility. A significant escalation in the federal role with respect to objectives would be the specification of actual targets for each of these objectives. Only the Nielson Task Force has dared to broach the subject to this point, but it is perhaps not as silly as it sounds, particularly with respect to targets for student accessibility or training as outputs. The question should not be dismissed by provincial governments and universities; after all, the Canada Health Act sets specific conditions for the health component of EPF transfers.

The federal agenda has gone beyond looking for a seat at the table and a share in setting objectives and limiting the decision-making autonomy of universities to requiring some accountability for federal funds used in post-secondary education. There has been no suggestion to this point that the Auditor General of Canada undertake an audit of federal EPF transfers, and the evolution of an increasing audit role is much more likely, to occur at the provincial level. What may be more likely, is some form of reporting by universities or provincial governments to the federal government on the use of post-secondary funding—in effect, accountability representations by the recipients of transfers.

The Parliamentary Task Force in 1981 urged that federal ministers receive from provincial administrators the information necessary to account to Parliament for the federal resources allocated to post-secondary education. An amendment to the Established Programmes Financing legislation (Bill C-12) in 1984 was unanimously accepted by all parties in the House of Commons, and required the Secretary of State to make an annual report to Parliament dealing with the following matters: first, the federal cash contributions and transfers to each province; second, provincial expenditures on post-secondary education; third, other federal programmes supporting higher education; fourth, the relationship between federal transfers and programmes and Canada's educational and economic goals; and finally, the results of any consultations by or on behalf of the Secretary of State with the Council of Ministers of Education, Canada relating to the definition of national purposes to be served by post-secondary education and the means by which the governments of Canada and the provinces would achieve these purposes. This report was required to be submitted to Parliament each year, beginning in 1986, and is referred to a standing committee of the House of Commons for consideration. The unanimous acceptance of the amendment requiring this report indicates concern felt at the federal level, and suggests that an approach by universities, almost certainly through provincial governments—and perhaps, indeed, through the Council of Ministers of Education—to reporting to Parliament might alleviate federal concern and remove some of the instability and uncertainty of federal funding.

In Australia, the Commonwealth government and the state governments have agreed on the national purposes of post-secondary education, and have agreed on complete federal funding through an intermediary body—the Tertiary Education Commission. In Canada, constitutional constraints, and the role of Quebec in particular, preclude this solution. The fact remains, however, that the federal government pays 80 per cent of the operating costs of universities in Canada and 60 per cent of the direct research costs. The trump card which the federal government holds is unquestionably the level of funding and its capacity to influence the adequacy and stability of that level. But this is a crude weapon. The evolution of the debate suggests that the federal government would prefer to ensure adequacy and stability in its general funding role in return for some form of matching provincial commitment to funding; federal participation in the establishment of national purposes for post-secondary education—particularly those relating to quality and accessibility; some form of reasonable accountability reporting perhaps through the Council of Ministers of Education; and assurances to Parliament that funds transferred to the provinces with respect to post-secondary education provide value for money.

Perspective of the Provincial Governments

The story of university independence and alleged government interference is difficult to unravel in any one province; with ten provincial governments to consider, the tale is obviously too long for this paper. The essentials are these:

- Provincial governments have operated through a variety of intermediary granting councils or agencies—either advisory or executive, based on delegated decision-making authority—to determine the size and distribution of operating and capital grants to universities, and in some cases to decide on approval of new degree programmes proposed by the universities. These grants have been in the form of block allocations—there has been no formal earmarking of operating funds, though there may have been informal leadership in government speeches about university priorities.

    Since the mid-1970s some of these intermediary agencies have been removed, either because government wants more direct control or because universities themselves have lobbied for their removal (as in the province of British Columbia).

- This general granting mode has not so far been replaced by any formal contractual mode. In no case in Canada have either competitive bids for delivery of university services or simple contracts for delivery of university services, been required by governments.

- As noted, the federal government cannot require—and provincial governments have not (so far) required—detailed information prior to making grants—except for new programmes which must demonstrate 'need'.

- Only data on student numbers and financial costs per student have normally been required of universities in reporting on performance.

On funding levels, however, provincial governments have definitely displayed a willingness to crack the whip. It can be argued that financial constraints have resulted in part from the failure of universities to tell their story effectively, through provision of adequate planning and budgeting information, and ex-post reporting on performance. If there is any evidence that universities are well-managed institutions pursuing goals reflecting public priorities, it is evidence well-hidden. But whatever the reason, and in spite of universities perceiving financial constraints as being severe, they do not seem to have been willing to depart much from 'business as usual' in response.

The result has been frustration both in provincial legislatures and among the public. From this frustration has sprung pressure to insist on greater legislative scrutiny through 'value for money audits', reporting either on the simple existence of management systems in place to address accountability, or indeed on the performance indicators themselves.

One response to this frustration, and growing concerns with the structure of the post-secondary system more generally, has been to create within the provincial Council of Ministers of Education, Canada, a ministerial post-secondary education sub-committee. This committee, an outgrowth of the National Forum on Post-Secondary Education, has initiated some work to develop coordinated provincial statistical systems and data bases, with the intention of developing some coordinated assessment of quality and effectiveness.

Enthusiasm within the university community has not, to date, been overwhelming.

Conclusions

The argument of this note can be summarized in two general conclusions:

1. Universities in Canada face a variety of pressures from government funders. Pressures prior to funding include information required of universities by government, information governing the use of resources prescribed as conditions on funding by governments to universities, and general constraints on funding levels. Pressures after the money has been provided relate to a broader scope of accountability including value for money, and include accountability reports by, and external

audits of, universities required by governments. The set of pressures can be likened to a five-sided vise squeezing in on the autonomy and discretion of the institution.

2. Universities may choose to ignore these pressures or to respond by providing incomplete or inaccurate or incomprehensible information. They may also respond cooperatively in a passive way by complying with funding and other conditions, and by providing whatever information is required, or may go further to shape the information agenda by designing and providing to funders more and better information than is actually required of them.

University response is a matter of choice. A positive approach is possible, based on the following line of argument.

1. Simply ignoring the increasing financial pressures and growing concern for accountability would exacerbate the situation and place the survival of universities in Canada as relatively autonomous institutions in serious jeopardy. The experience of British universities under the Education Reform Bill of late-1987 is instructive. Non-cooperation through inaccurate or incomplete information would have the same consequences.

2. Non-cooperation by 'smothering' funders with incomprehensible and unusable data might divert the pressures in the short run but would probably exacerbate them in the long.

3. A cooperative response of a passive nature is the least that funding agencies can expect of universities, and the minimal pre-requisite to any alleviation of external pressures. However, such a response leaves the agenda of information prescriptions and requirements entirely in the hands of funders. That agenda is therefore unlikely to reflect accurately the circumstances and performance of universities and, moreover, will be driven by changing political preferences and will therefore be highly unstable.

4. An active cooperative response to external pressures by universities, on the other hand, will enable them to shape the information agenda to their advantage—at the very least, having it reflect reasonably accurately their circumstances and performance—and to control its evolution. Universities will therefore enjoy a more stable environment. Further, active cooperation would likely reduce the severity and frequency of both conditions on funding and on reporting and auditing requirements. Also, by demonstrating that what is spent is well

spent, cooperation might contribute to more generous funding levels.

This last observation is based on the premise that much of the expectations gap—the gap between what external funders want and what they perceive universities to be doing—reflects the inability or unwillingness of universities to provide thorough and useful information on what they are doing. It is also likely that the information presently collected internally can, suitably adjusted and wrapped, satisfy many of the external demands, but that some creative new information will also be necessary. It is also probably inevitable that universities will actually have to do some different things and report on them. But clarifying this communications gap will help to identify those necessary behaviourial changes which may not prove inconsistent with the universities' own basic purposes or interests.

5. The legitimate concerns of funders about accountability can best be addressed by the development of a reporting framework of the following kind. Universities should provide to funders information in the form of performance budgets (similar to Part III of the Estimates of the Government of Canada), and in the form of annual accountability reports which provide detailed accounts of how the terms of reference set out in the budgets have been addressed. Faced with such evidence, funders could then require of external auditors that they simply attest to the completeness and accuracy of annual reports by universities (and thus avoid the necessity of cadres of accountants attempting to develop questionable methodologies to deal with inappropriate applications in unfamiliar circumstances).

6. Universities acting together can produce a better reporting package than universities acting separately. Indeed, unless universities act together, funders have no information (from the university perspective) about the performance of the university system as a whole. Such co-operation should include the design of inter-institutional resource allocation criteria which would otherwise be determined by funders. The trick in such essential cooperative action will be to preserve the necessary and important competition among universities for students and research funds.

7. Meaningful and useful information of the sort required for budget submissions and reporting can be produced by universities. Universities are complex multiple-product organizations, but the state-of-the-art in management systems, and in

defining and measuring resource utilisation and the attainment of objectives, is such that sufficient evidence can be produced to satisfy the reasonable expectations of funders. Addressing the problem seriously is also the shortest route to improving the state-of-the-art. What seems clear is that the information produced in budgets and reports is likely to be far better if universities produce it themselves than if it is designed and produced by some external agency—government ministry, central agency, or external auditor.

8. The new information produced by universities will be useful to decision-makers on the funding of universities, and will make a difference to those decisions. Universities must compete for their share in the allocation of scarce resources. The more complete and persuasive the information presented, the better will universities do in the competition for scarce resources at the margin. This strong premise is based on the arguments that universities actually do much that is expected of them as a recipient of public subvention, but are generally bad at demonstrating this stewardship (4, above) and that the state-of-the-art is such that more and better information can be produced than at present (7, above).

9. The new information cannot be produced without cost, but that cost is relatively small, and is not material compared to the benefits universities will enjoy as a consequence, though these are difficult to identify and impute. If the investment resulted in improved funding levels, the case is obvious. Less obvious, but perhaps even more important would be gains, or the avoidance of losses, in decision-making autonomy, or in the opportunity to design the presentation of accountability reporting. The question of avoidance of loss is not trivial. In this, as in so much public policy, the *status quo* is not an option. Universities must move to control the agenda, and to ease the pressures on the vise; the alternative is the progressive erosion of decision-making autonomy and a very different and much less vital university sector in Canada.

10. Part of the cost will be new institutions and new information-gathering and evaluation methods and staff in universities. These new institutions, methods and staff will have to find appropriate recognition in a university system in which to date they are relatively novel, even alien.

11. Funders must also change, tempering their expectations about information and behaviour, and providing universities with the

incentives and the opportunities to plan, behave, and report in accordance with reasonable expectations.

In comparison with the experience in the United Kingdom, Australia, and the United States, Canadian universities have taken a bit of a beating on funding levels, but have emerged almost unscathed in terms of financial control (earmarking of funds, contracting of services) or accountability requirements (detailed reporting, external 'value for money' audit). For universities, a window of opportunity appears to be open to shape the agenda and, perhaps, to disarm the funding weapon while meeting legitimate public concerns for greater candour and accountability. The approach would combine improved planning and budgeting submissions, fuller reporting of information and systems already in place and of new information from new internal audit systems, the whole reporting structure to be designed at two levels, first, for individual institutions, and, second, the university systems in each province. Some approach to reporting to the federal government also needs to be developed, perhaps through the provincial council of ministers of education.

In sum, if there is to be a future for universities in Canada as relatively autonomous, independent institutions, it will probably lie somewhat along these lines so far as governance and accountability are concerned. It will also entail universities adjusting their activities more than they have seemed willing to do to date—but that is a different paper.

Annex A

This annex examines the evolution of the various components of the framework of control by governments over universities and argues that the development of improved management decision-making systems and controls and a more careful response to accountability reporting are needed in Canada to avert radical intervention by government of the sort visited upon universities in the United Kingdom.

Figure 2 outlines the dimensions of the question. The various instruments of control available to government are set out as the row headings; these instruments are directed at two broad categories of target—limiting the decision-making autonomy of universities, and increasing their accountability. The two broad dimensions illustrated in Figure 2 are considered in turn.

The first instrument of control relates to structures. It is assumed in all cases that governments exert indirect control through the appointment of a majority of members of boards of governors of universities. The distinction is then drawn between indirect and direct structural control. In the former, government acts through an appointed intermediary agency in its dealings with universities and, in the latter, such dealings are conducted directly by a ministry of government. Structural response by universities may involve independent or joint action in their dealings with governments.

Given structure, and thus the line of communication used by government, information requirements and prescriptions are divided into those imposed prior to and after funding, and the actual level of funding itself. Information required of universities prior to funding includes a variety of levels of detail in planning and budgeting information, and implies—or may even be extended to include an explicit statement about—management systems, controls, and practices sufficient to produce valid and reliable information of the sort required. Ex-ante information prescriptions include various sets of general and specific conditions attached to funding, and again imply or may require explicitly that management systems, controls, and practices be in place to comply with such conditions. The aggregate level of funding itself is the bluntest and most obvious instrument of direct control. Its impact on the administration of universities will also be affected by the time horizon over which funding commitments by government are made; indeed, the capacity of universities to respond to controls will be greatly increased if funding levels, regardless of their perceived adequacy, are predictable over, say, a three to five year time horizon.

Figure 2
Control Instruments and Targets

Targets of Control / Instruments of Control	Decision-making Autonomy								Accountability							
	Ends				Means				Procedural		Consequential					
	Long-Term		Short-Term		Capital		Operating		Finan-cial	Compli-ance	Economy & Efficiency		Effective-ness		Cost-Effectiveness	
	Direct	Indirect	Direct	Indirect	Direct	Indirect	Direct	Indirect			Direct	Indirect	Direct	Indirect	Direct	Indirect
1. Structure a) Intermediary b) Direct																
2. Information Requirements and Prescriptions																
(a) Ex-ante Requirements																
(a) Ex-ante Prescriptions																
(b) Level of Funding																
(c) Ex-post Report Requirements																
(c) Ex-post Audit Requirements																

After providing funding, governments may require of universities—individually, and/or collectively—reports of various kinds and frequency on the use of funds and the results obtained. The degree of control exercised through such requirements for 'accountability statements' or management representations will be greater, the greater the complexity and/or the frequency of report requirements. Equally, the meaningfulness of such ex-ante controls as may have been imposed will depend on the response by universities to such controls through some form of ex-post accountability. Governments invariably require that universities produce annually a set of financial statements to which the accuracy and completeness an independent external auditor must attest. Universities may also be subject to an additional external audit of their compliance with legislative and statutory authorities. Most important, governments or legislative auditors may choose to subject universities, individually or collectively, to a broader scope audit of varying frequency and degrees of comprehensiveness related to the utilization of resources and results obtained.

The various instruments of control are directed either at reducing autonomy in decision-making by universities or at improving accountability, somehow defined, for the use of scarce public resources by universities. The generic target may be considered to be value for money. In essence, controls are directed at the ends pursued by universities, the means used to pursue these ends, the associated resources utilized, and the results achieved. Value for money can also be defined to go beyond educational and economic matters to include such matters as access to university places by students and employees.

The column headings in Figure 2 set out illustrative specific targets. The question of autonomy in decision-making is divided into autonomy with respect to ends and means. Ends are divided into long-term and short-term ends, each in turn treated either directly or indirectly. This represents interest by government in long-term or planning objectives, over, say, a three to five year period, and/or in short-term or operational objectives over, say, one academic year, and either direct specification by government of what these objectives must be or, much milder, indirect specification of a requirement that universities have systems in place to establish such objectives. Given the inevitability of multiple objectives in universities, governments may also specify priorities among these objectives or require that universities specify them, may specify or insist that universities specify operational measures by which the attainment of objectives can be determined, and may also specify, or require the specification of, actual performance targets for the set of objectives.

It is perhaps worth pausing briefly on this question of objectives, for objectives are, in logic if not always in practice, the centrepiece of the target of government control. Public funding of universities reflects the view that broad public objectives relating to such matters as economic growth, the quality of life, and fairness or equity, can be serve better than any other way through the pursuit of the objectives of research, teaching and public service in universities. In a hierarchical sense it is this 'value' part which takes precedence in value for money. It is important to be efficient, that is, to be 'doing the thing right' (pursuing objectives at least cost); it is clearly a prior consideration to be effective, that is, to be 'doing the right thing'. From the perspective of public funders 'doing the right thing' is more than pursuing performance targets in teaching and research. It relates to broader issues of relevance, appropriateness, acceptance by constituencies or customers, and responsiveness to changing demands (Canadian Comprehensive Auditing Foundation, *Effectiveness: Reporting and Auditing in the Public Sector* (Ottawa: Canadian Comprehensive Auditing Foundation, 1987)). This larger perspective of 'quality' or the value ascribed by funders, reflecting public views, to the results achieved by universities (P. Bourke, *Quality Measures in Universities* (Canberra, Australia: Commonwealth Tertiary Education Commission, 1986)), provides a context for the narrower and more tractable—though still difficult—perspective of the quality of teaching and research outcomes. One dimension of such quality broadly defined can be estimated in monetary terms: the productivity and corresponding income gains enjoyed by graduates or users of research. The broad concept of quality from the perspective of funders may also, as noted above, be defined to include special questions of access to universities in terms, say, of age, sex, ethnic group, and geographic location, and may go further to deal with the consequences for income and wealth distribution of public funding of universities; the question of who benefits and who pays is of central significance where direct beneficiaries assume a small portion of the costs and enjoy a large portion of the benefits. In short, the question of effectiveness is likely to be complex, multi-dimensional, difficult to conceptualize let alone measure, and to present particular difficulties of translation from the level of general public intentions, as articulated by funders, to the particular activities and outcomes of universities, and therefore also to present difficulties of monitoring and accountability.

Funders may also seek to influence the means by which universities pursue their objectives. Influence may be exerted on both capital and operating activities, again either directly by specification or indirectly by requiring that universities have management systems in place to deal with these matters. Influence on operating activities is of particular interest, and funders may actually earmark funds in various levels of detail by academic or support programme, and/or by broad functions such as teaching and research. In the strongest and most direct form of intervention, funders could actually specify programme design and budget breakdown. At the milder end of the spectrum, indirect intervention could take the form of a requirement by funders that universities have in place management systems and associated resource allocation criteria for dividing the operating budget among programmes. The more direct and specific the detail of the intervention, the greater the reduction in the autonomy of universities in decision-making.

The second set of targets defined as the column headings in Figure 2 are grouped under the head of accountability, defined in relation to ongoing and/or retrospective reporting by university management (which may build on internal audit) and external audit of university management. The concept is defined in Figure 2 to include procedural and consequential accountability. The former includes financial accountability—a requirement to provide a complete and accurate financial accounting of the use of public funds—and compliance—the requirement to comply with the various statutory and regulatory authorities associated with public funding. As for reductions in autonomy and decision-making by universities, funders may insist on a direct representation or audit or may be satisfied with indirect accountability, that is, with representations or audit on the management systems, controls, and—of central importance in retrospective assessment—actual management practices which show due regard for procedural accountability. Increasing interest by funders in accountability is, of course, directed at consequential accountability which refers to the retrospective aspect of value for money. The main categories of consequential accountability are illustrated in Figure 2. The first category includes economy and efficiency: the former is defined as economy in the acquisition of resources, and is a building block of efficiency in resource utilisation, formally defined as the ratio of resources used to some standard output or activity measure. The second category refers to measures of effectiveness, defined as the extent to which the objectives of publicly funded programmes have been achieved; in discussing limitations on decision-making autonomy in universities, it was pointed out that effectiveness has to be seen in terms of a complex range or hierarchy of measures which reflect the perceived 'quality' of university outcomes, and social indicators related to such questions as student access. The final category links costs with effectiveness and benefit. The former requires the matching of a measure of resource utilisation with one or more measures of effectiveness; the latter obtains when the output measure matched with cost is defined in dollar terms (such as income gains attributable to university education) in which case the matching can be the basis of what is commonly referred to as rate of return analysis or, with some analytical adjustments, cost-benefit analysis. Figure 2 indicates that, as for procedural accountability, consequential accountability may be approached indirectly by representation or audit on the systems, controls, and practices with which management discharges its responsibility, or directly by representations or audit on the actual operating results attained by management. Obviously, direct representations or audit on operating results represents a higher order of accountability than indirect representations or audit, and the accountability required of management may also be considered more onerous the more complex the definition of value for money that is required—for instance, representations or audit dealing with the matching of costs and a range of effectiveness measures would be considerably more complex than representations or audit confined, say, to economy in purchasing or efficiency in the utilisation of resources.

IV

OPEN AND DISTANCE EDUCATION

The Open College of South London: A Development in Post-School Education

MARGARET BIRD
   RESEARCHER, INNER LONDON EDUCATION AUTHORITY

Mr. Kenneth Baker, the British Education Secretary, called for increased access to higher education 'for women, ethnic minorities, poorer people and older students' at Lancaster University on January 6th, 1989.[1] The speech marks, once again, the stated aim of central government to open up education to a wider clientele. This intention has been manifest in initiatives sponsored by central government, the most notable examples of which have been the development of the Open University and the locally delivered adult literacy programme. Into the obvious gap between these two levels of provision stepped some initiatives sponsored by local education authorities who administer the education service (other than the university sector) under the auspices of local government. This paper is concerned with one such initiative, the Open College of South London,[2] which is a consortium of educational institutions in the post-school sector in the locality of South London. The objective of the Open College of South London was to create pathways for adult returners to higher education, or to vocational courses and more immediately the field of employment.

There are a number of similarities between Britain and Canada that make this initiative a subject of common interest: both countries face an overall decline in the number of school leavers and therefore have institutions with falling rolls in the non-advanced sector of post-school education (in Canada, community colleges, and in Britain, colleges of further education); the economies of both are growing and there is an increasing demand for technological skills in the labour market at a time when the unskilled and semi-skilled workers find it increasingly difficult to find employment; and, therefore, it appears both will have to make more effective use of their labour potential in the adult population if the economy is to continue to grow. The noticeable difference between the two countries is that Britain has a significantly smaller proportion of the post-school population entering further education (30 per cent compared to Canada's 45 per cent) although it had, until quite recently, a much more developed system of apprenticeship training than Canada, where there has been a dependence on the skills of immigrant labour.[3] There are, nevertheless, indications in both countries that there are amongst the adult population a substantial number of people, noticeably women and ethnic minority groups, who missed out on education for one reason or another and would, perhaps, welcome the opportunity to return to education on a number of counts, not least because they are unemployed (or under-employed).

The purpose of this paper is to examine the 1983 development of one such initiative, The Open College of South London, which was designed to address these needs. By placing the case study within the general framework of the social, economic and political system and employing theories concerning the implementation of social policy, it is hoped that it may enable some comparisons to be drawn with similar developments elsewhere in Britain and, perhaps, in Canada. Whilst some translation of terminology may be needed, the nature of organisations, the role of professionals within educational institutions and the factors influencing policy implementation, it is suggested, do not differ substantially from one western country to another. The perspective and concepts employed to understand organisations are universal in their application.[4] In broad terms, the implementation issue most straightforwardly concerns how, in the words of Walter Williams, to bring together 'communication, commitment and capacity so as to carry a decision into action'.[5] In testing this hypothesis in relation to the Open College of South London, therefore, it is hoped that some lessons may be learned from this one experience in developing opportunities in the post-school field which may be of value elsewhere. First, let us trace the origins of this initiative by a local education authority and examine the economic, social and political context in which it took place.

The Historical Background to the 'Open College' Development: The Gradual Expansion of Educational Opportunities

One can trace the gradual expansion of educational opportunities over a long period since the Education Act of 1870.[6] Notwithstanding this gradual extension of the educational franchise it was recognised in the 1960s that there was a substantial proportion of the population whose capabilities had not been fully developed[7] and, on grounds of social justice, it was argued by some that the expansion of education was desirable in order to ensure greater equality of outcomes.[8] Such a policy was also recommended in terms of the needs of the then expanding economy, and it was, perhaps, this argument which had the most political impact.[9] When, in the 1970s, it became evident that a decline in birth rate would result in spare capacity in post-16 education, it was proposed to open up and systematise the opportunities for mature students.[10] Social groups which were identified as likely to have benefitted least from the education system were immigrant women, the handicapped and the children of manual workers. But because there has, generally, been an inverse relationship between demand and need in adult education,[11] these groups, traditionally, have not acted as a pressure group on central government. Overall, there was no effective co-ordination of the interests of educationally disadvantaged groups within the adult population at a national level, although the National Institute of Adult Education had highlighted in a number of studies[12] the educational needs of adults and the inadequate nature of provision at that time. Central government took two measures to meet the needs of educationally disadvantaged groups in the 1970s: the first was to grant 'paid release' for the training of workplace representatives following pressure from the trade-union movement;[13] and the second was to allocate a substantial sum of money over a three-year period for the Adult Literacy Campaign.[14] This, perhaps, had more to do with the needs of the economy and labour market than with arguments concerning social justice. During the 1970s, the central government was subject to international pressure[15] and it commissioned a survey on paid educational leave (PEL).[16] By 1979, however, the year in which the this commission reported, the impact of the economic recession was clearly evident. A Conservative Government was returned in the general election of that year and education spending suffered a two per cent cut in line with public expenditure reduction as a whole. The macro-economic and political situation in the late 1970s, therefore, was not favourable to the expansion of educational opportunities. It was left to local education authorities to respond to the needs of the identifiable educationally disadvantaged groups in the population.

There were a number of events in the 1970s which served to raise the awareness of socially disadvantaged adults of the possible benefits to be gained from adult education/training: equal opportunity issues in employment heightened women's concern with the discrepancies in pay and the underlying inequality in training available;[17] the 'Black Power' movement raised the consciousness of ethnic minority groups of the educational disadvantages suffered by their children;[18] and a government committee of enquiry into the education of handicapped children revealed the disadvantage suffered by this group.[19] By the late 1970s the voices of certain politically aware groups (women and ethnic minorities) began to be heard on local councils. The social deprivation of the inner city population manifested itself, in its extreme form, in the Brixton riots of 1981. When the Labour Party won control of the Greater London Council in 1981 it had a manifesto which was committed to tackling social inequalities and the Inner London Education Authority launched a policy initiative on equal opportunities on race, sex and class. This was the social and local political context in which the 'Open College' was conceived.

The Inner London Educational Authority is a large unitary authority serving a population of nearly two and a half million.[20] In common with other large conurbations the inner city is high on all indices of social deprivation: poor housing; and a large proportion of large families, one-parent families and those in receipt of supplementary benefit. It also has the highest proportion of non-white population of any city in Britain (it is estimated that 20 per cent of the population in inner London are non-white). In terms of additional educational needs, as measured by the Department of Education and Science the Inner London Educational Authority was assessed as the local education authority most in need. It had already responded to a number of central government commissions[21] and following a survey of adult education in connection with the Russell Report (1973),[22] it set up a working party on continuing education to explore ways of making adult education more accessible to the educationally disadvantaged sections of the population. It also expanded opportunities for non-standard entry to its polytechnics, by developing 'access' courses in adult education institutes and colleges of further education and by making some full-time maintenance awards to adult students.

Aware of the changing demography within the inner city, the Authority conducted a major review of advanced further education.[23] This report recommended that access to higher education be facilitated for groups who were under-represented by creating a 'ladder of opportunity' through the promotion of 'geographic groupings of institutions which would list access in a systematic way'.[24] Whilst the report was not published until 1984, senior officers were engaged in the process of consultation with institutions for some long time prior to publication. It was the organisational context in which the 'Open College' was conceived.

Policy-making

It is clear that there were a number of factors operating simultaneously within the Inner London Educational Authority: the chief education officer, appointed in 1982, had instituted a formal review of advanced further education; the newly-elected members of the Greater London Council had a manifesto concerned with equal opportunities;[25] and the educational institutions in further and higher education were increasingly concerned with falling rolls. Meanwhile the cuts in spending by central government were looming on the horizon and the polytechnic concerned in this study in South London was informed by a senior officer that if it did not pay more attention to the needs of the local community its grant would be reduced. It is, perhaps, not unconnected with this, that the political adviser to the director of the polytechnic undertook an entrepreneurial initiative in relation to the local colleges of further education and adult education institutes (AEIs), sounding out the notion of an 'Open College', which he had seen developed in the north-west.[26] At the same time, he sought to develop interest and support for the idea within the polytechnic.

Within certain local colleges and institutes there was some experience of collaboration in course development and a history, therefore, of co-operative working. Institutions were attracted by the notion of establishing more systematic routes in order for their mature students to progress through the post-school system, but were somewhat fearful that the polytechnic was also mounting a take-over bid which would threaten the autonomy of their institutions. Fears were allayed, in part, in the ensuing negotiations and a steering group was formed which sought the support of senior officers and leading members of the education committee. It was agreed that half the resources would be provided by the Authority and the other half would be provided by the institutions from within their existing budgets.

It would be erroneous to suggest, however, that the 'Open College' development was undertaken purely on grounds of expediency, for there was a strong commitment within adult education to the expansion of provision for the least educationally advantaged adults on moral grounds. An interest in development in the post-school sector was present within the institutions for a number of reasons which fitted with the administrators' requirement to review the service and with the politicians (members) interest in equal opportunities for particular groups. If, as suggested, successful formulation of policy requires 'commitment, communication and capacity',[27] it would appear that the proposal for an 'Open College' was timely. The initiative was launched in November 1983.

The Implementation of Policy

The 'Open College' was, therefore, not an institution as such, but a consortium of further education colleges, adult education institutes and a polytechnic with a central administrative unit, based in a small site belonging to the polytechnic.[28] It comprised a director of studies, who was the former political adviser to the director, and four central co-ordinators, each with a responsibility for course development and liaison between institutions in a particular field (access, return to learning, new technology and open learning). Within each of the 14 member institutions there was a co-ordinator who had 40-50 per cent remission from teaching in order to liaise within and between institutions with a view to course development in the four designated areas. A joint planning board was set up to meet termly, comprising a senior member of management from each institutions, two representatives of the central team, four representatives of the institutions co-ordinators, two from further education and two from adult education. The aim was states as:

> Promoting close collaboration between institutions of Higher, Further and Adult Education in providing access to designated programmes for those mature students (19+) who have benefited least from existing education provision.
>
> These programmes will fulfil one or more of the following criteria. They will: be intended primarily for mature students (19+); have no formal entry requirements; offer alternatives to traditional single subject public examinations; offer flexible hours and means of attendance; facilitate attendance by making creche and playgroups available and by making provision for disabled students; enable students to progress to more advanced courses where appropriate; be socially and educationally relevant to the students and involve them in the design of the schemes of work.

Certain factors can be identified from the studies of the implementation of policy elsewhere which may help to promote the successful outcome of policy initiatives. It has been noted that a history of innovation in an institution can create a climate favourable to change;[29] that the dominant values of the institution, the organisational culture, influences the climate;[30] that the measure of internal or external support available may be influential (the role of a change-agent may be helpful);[31] that the allocation of resources, even the timing, may be critical;[32] and that good avenues of communication are important.[33] As in the case of policy-formulation, therefore, the implementation issue most straightforwardly concerns how to bring together 'communications, commitment and capacity so as to carry a decision into action'.[34] This hypothesis was, therefore, tested against the experience of the central team and against that of the principals and co-ordinators in the member institutions.[35]

The Central Team

A detailed study of the experiences of those concerned revealed that there were differences in the efficacy of members of the central team in promoting course development in the four designated areas: the most dramatic expansion of course development took place in the area of 'return to learning' and 'access' provision; the least successful was the field of 'open learning'.

In testing the hypothesis that implementation concerned communication, commitment and capacity, it was found that all these factors were important to the success of the 'Open College' development, but that the problem for central staff was that they had no jurisdiction or control of the staff responsible for courses in the institutions; equally, the member institutions felt they could not exercise any control over the roles of the central co-ordinators through the Joint Planning Board. Therefore, overall, the Open College of South London suffered from a lack of direction. The Joint Planning Board was vexed over questions relating to institutional autonomy; it did not have a shared view owing to the culture schism between the interests of colleges of advanced education and colleges of further education.[36]

The ability of the central co-ordinators to influence development was entirely dependent on their ability to communicate and to provide a forum for supporting lecturers in the development of the curriculum and course materials in the designated areas; they had to negotiate their role with the staff in the member institutions. The co-ordinators for 'return to learning' and 'access' provision were helped in this because they were more likely to share a common subject background in the social science/arts with the co-ordinators in the institutions as well as having had previous experience of working in these areas. Links were successfully developed by staff which enabled adult students to progress from 'return to learning' to 'access' courses and into higher education, vocational education or employment.

The Member Institution

Some institutions were much more effective than others in meeting the needs of educationally disadvantaged adults. The most successful development, in terms of new courses and student progression, took place where key people (the principal and institution's co-ordinator) were committed to the development of the curriculum for adult returners; where the institution had suitable resources; and where good communications existed between the institutional co-ordinator and the central co-ordinator of the 'Open College'. Space precludes a detailed evaluation of the four designated areas of course development. Given below, is a summary of a longitudinal study of one of the areas concerned.[37]

An Evaluation of Introductory Courses in New Technology

Performance criteria by which an 'Open College' might be judged were identified as: the recruitment of adults who were educationally disadvantaged; the provision of courses which met the needs of adult returners; and the extent to which people went on to take further courses or found employment. Overall, the longitudinal study revealed that colleges/institutes were recruiting from among the disadvantaged section of the population (women, ethnic minorities, and those with few, if any, qualifications); people were generally wanting to improve their career prospects or progress to courses at a higher level. Important factors in determining enrolment were that people could afford the course fees and that the college/institute was near to where they lived or worked.

Evaluation revealed considerable variation between institutions in meeting the needs of adult students. The differences in efficacy were related to: the commitment of principals in making the resources available; the interest of the co-ordinators in developing the curriculum and establishing links with other institutions to facilitate progression; and the sensitivity of course tutors to the particular needs of adult students so that they developed the requisite study skills and self-confidence.

Summary

The study set out to identify the important conditions required for opening up post-school education to mature adults in the population. It revealed that the 'Open College' was, in part, a supply-led initiative by educational institutions to reach a wider clientele because they were faced with falling rolls; it was, also, an innovation relevant to the economic and social needs of Inner London at the time.

Successful implementation required that at each level of operation key people were committed to the development, that they could communicate effectively with others in the network and that institutions had the capacity to deliver courses.

Discussion

What can be learned from the implementation of an 'Open College' which might be of value in Canada? All levels of government, or so it would appear, are seeking new ways of making post-school education more accessible to a wider section of the population.[38] A cursory glance, too, at some of the recent literature[39] suggests some interesting parallels with Britain; technological development, economic recession and demographic change means that institutions face a period of rationalisation. Post-secondary institutions in Canada are facing the same issues: Ontario's community colleges are looking for 'better ways to serve and ensure access for special communities and disadvantaged adults'; and British Columbia is, also, evaluating access to post-secondary education in the province.[40]

The experience in South London demonstrates that where there is commitment, capacity and communication, it is possible to develop new curricula, to facilitate progression between courses and institutions and to recruit adults from among the more socially disadvantaged groups in the population. It would appear that, in forming a consortium, particular attention needs to be paid to the questions of communication, control and the possibility of conflict arising from different organisational cultures. However, comparisons with educational provision in other parts of London show that more has been accomplished by an 'Open College' than has been achieved by institutions acting in isolation; each type of institution, with its own history and culture, has its own unique contribution to make to adult returners. The experience in South London suggests that institutions, while conceding some control over staff and resources to the consortium, retain overall institutional autonomy which has certain advantages for local communities. This can help to ensure that institutions are sensitive and responsive to the needs of their locality.

It can be appreciated that governments, both local and national (in Canada, provincial and federal), may have good economic reasons to influence developments in the post-school sector. In considering a whole range of initiatives, it would be unwise to overlook the expertise and experience that already resides within the system. Quite modest measures (in relation to fees, student grants, loans and creche facilities) could have a substantial impact upon the opening up of the full-range of educational courses to a wider section of the population. This would enable people, on a full-time or part-time basis, to combine education with family, work and other commitments.

Notes

1. The speech by Mr. Kenneth Baker, the Education Secretary, was made at a conference on Higher Education at Lancaster University on January 5th 1989. *The Guardian*, 6th January 1989.

2. The 'Open College of South London' is not to be confused with the 'Open College' sponsored by central government in 1987 to provide vocational courses, by 'distance learning' and 'open learning' mechanisms, using the services provided by colleges in both the public and private sector. Early indications, based on observation, indicate that the 'Open College' is not recruiting the large numbers of students envisaged and that the mediums of 'distance' and 'open learning' are, perhaps, not attractive or appropriate for the more educationally disadvantaged section of the population.

3. Robertson, Nickerson, Group Associates Limited, *Case Studies on Aspects of Training Upper Skilled Blue-Collar Industrial Workers* (Department of Employment and Immigration, Ottawa, 1978). The survey found 73 per cent of skilled craftsmen were born outside of Canada.

4. The study uses both a 'systems' approach employing the Easton model of decision-making found in D.A. Easton, *A Systems Analysis of Political Life* (New York and London, Wiley, 1965) and the 'social action' perspective as discussed in D. Silverman, *Qualitative Methodology and Sociology* (Gower, Aldershot, 1985).

5. W. Williams *The Implementation Perspective: a guide for managing social delivery programs* (Berkeley, University of California Press, 1980), p. 3.

6. Harold Silver advocates the examination of social forces influencing policy formulation over a fairly long period in order to fathom the 'dialectic of ideas and behaviour'. H. Silver, *Education as History* (London and New York, Methuen, 1983).

7. J. Floyd, A.H. Halsey, C. Arnold Anderson, *Economy and Society: a Reader in the Sociology of Education* (London, MacMillan, 1961). Also, J.W.B. Douglas, *The Home and the School: A Study of Ability and Attainment in the Primary School* (London, MacGibbon and Kee, 1964) among others.

8. H. Glennerster, 'Education and Inequality' in P. Townsend and N. Bosanquet, *Labour and Inequality* (London, Fabian Society, 1972).

9. M. Blaug, *Economics of Education I* (Harmondsworth, Penguin Modern Economics, 1968). Also the major government commissions: Crowther (1959), Newsom (19634), Robbins (1963), Plowden (1967).

10. *Education: A Framework for Expansion* Cmnd 5174 (London, HMSO, 1972). Also, *Higher Education for the 1990s. A Discussion Document* (London, HMSO, 1978).

11. K. Rubenson, 'Adult Education and the Quality of Life', *Learning*, Vol. 3, No. 4 (1983).

12. The Association for Adult Continuing Education under the auspices if the National Institute of Adult Education (Leicester), published a number of studies: *A Strategy for the Basic Education of Adults* (1979), *Protecting the Future of Adult Education* (1981), *Continuing Education: From Policies to Practice* (1981) and *Adults: Their Educational Experience and Needs* (1982).

13. This right was granted under Section 57 of the Employment Protection Act 1975 (Section 27, 1978).

14. For three consecutive years (1975-78) the DES made one million pounds available for the 'Adult Literacy Agency'.

15. The International Labour Office Convention 140 concerning 'Paid Educational Leave' (1974) called upon each member state to 'formulate and apply a policy designed to promote by methods appropriate to material conditions and practice and by stages, if necessary' the granting of paid educational leave (Ghazzali, 1975).

16. J. Killeen and M. Bird, *Education and Work* (Leicester, NIAE, 1981).

17. Government legislation in relation to 'equal pay and sex discrimination' took place in 1975. In 1981, women's earnings were, overall, 74.8 per cent of that of men. In 1976 a women's rights rally took place at Alexandra Palace. A Working Women's Charter put forward practical demands for child care, maternity and paternity rights... equal educational opportunities. (International Marxist Group).

18. T. Carter, *Shattering Illusions* London, Lawrence and Wishart, 1986), p. 81.

19. HMSO *Special Educational Needs. Report of the Committee of Inquiry into the Education of Handicapped Children and Young People* Cmnd 7212 (London, HMSO, 1978).

20. At the time the 'Open College' was conceived in 1983, the Inner London Education Authority (ILEA) was an autonomous special committee of the Greater London Council (GLC). Any GLC Member who sat for an Inner London constituency was automatically a Member of the ILEA. In addition there were 13 nominees from the 12 Inner London Borough Councils and 17 non-elected people. In 1986 the GLC was abolished by central government and direct elections were held for the ILEA, whereby two representatives were elected from each parliamentary constituency to serve on the ILEA. In 1990 the central government will abolish the ILEA and the individual boroughs will assume responsibility for education.

21. Following the Government's White Paper on the 'Educational Needs of Immigrants' (1974) the ILEA appointed a team of inspectors for multi-ethnic education and, later, in response to the Warnock report it introduced advisers for special educational needs. See F. Morrell, 'Policy for Schools in Inner London' in G. Grace, *Education and the Inner City. Theory, History and Contemporary Practice* (London, Routledge and Kegan Paul, 1984).

22. ILEA *Report by the Working Party on the social structures of the student body of adult education institutes* (London, ILEA, 1984).

23. *Review of Advanced Further Education* (London, ILEA, 1984).

24. Ibid., p. 2.

25. One of the first requests of the ILEA Education Committee was to require the Authority's research and statistics branch to review the existing literature on educational inequalities. See

Race, Sex and Class. Achievement in Schools (London, ILEA, 1983).

26. K. Percy et al., *Post-Initial Education in the North-West of England* (Leicester, ACACE, 1983).

27. W. Williams, *The Implementation Perspective: a guide for managing social delivery programs* (Berkeley, University of California Press, 1982), p. 17.

28. The main focus of provision in each type of institution is as follows: a polytechnic is an institution of higher education which specialises in courses which have a vocational orientation; a college of further education provides non-advanced vocational courses largely for the post-16 group; and an institute of adult education (AEI) is concerned with courses of a recreational nature but, increasingly, it also provides adult basic education. For the changing role of AEIs, see M. Bird and A. Varlaam, *Changing Course. Community Education in Inner London* (London, ILEA, 1987).

29. Among others, see N. Gross, J. Giaquinta and M. Berstein *Implementing Organisational Innovations* (New York, Basic Books, 1971) p. 22.

30. S.B. Sarason, *The Culture of the School and the Problem of Change* (London, Allyn and Bacon, 1982).

31. E. Bardach refers to the presence of a 'fixer', *The Implementation Game* (Cambridge, MIT Press, 1977).

32. D.A. Mazmanian and P.A. Sabatier *Effective Policy Implementation* (Lexington, D.C. Heath and Co., 1981).

33. Williams (1980), op. cit., p. 3.

34. Williams (1980), op. cit., Ch. 5. Effective policy implementation requires that the aims and intentions of the policy are made operational and guidelines adhered to at each stage of the implementation.

35. In-depth interviews were conducted with the key people concerned: senior officer, inspectors, leading Members (politicians), the central co-ordinators, the former director of studies, and nine co-ordinators and six principals in the institutions.

36. Generally, it was noted that the interest of the AEIs was in access for adults to return to education. 'Progression', in their

terms, was measured in terms of students" growth in confidence and broadening of view, whereas, in FE, interest in access for adults was much more concerned with progression to an 'Access' course to higher education. 'Distance education' tended to favour developing methods of accreditation, whereas AE feared that such a development would make the courses less 'open'.

37. M. Bird, *The Open College of South London, A study of students taking courses in new technology* (London, ILEA, 1987).

38. M. Bird, 'Continuing Education: An Examination of the Trends in Western Canada and Britain', *British Journal of Canadian Studies*, Vol. 1., No. 1.

39. J.D. Wilson, ed., *Canadian Education in the 1980s* (Calgary, Alberta, Detslig Enterprises Ltd., (1981).
J.D. Dennison and P. Gallagher, *Canada's Community Colleges. A Critical Analysis* (Vancouver, University of British Columbia Press, 1986) reviewed by M. Bird in *British Journal of Canadian Studies* Vol. 2, No. 2.

40. 'Looking into the Future of Ontario's College System', *Newsletter* (Canadian Education Association, December 1988).
'Report on Education access released in BC', *Newsletter* (Canadian Education Association, January 1989).

Distance Learning and Management Education: Developments and Prospects in the United Kingdom

ROB PATON
SCHOOL OF MANAGEMENT, THE OPEN UNIVERSITY

Introduction

Distance education is a loose idea encompassing a range of techniques and approaches.[1] In practice, but not in principle, it is closely associated with the idea of open learning.[2] This paper reviews the diffusion of distance learning methods into management education in the United Kingdom and considers some of the issues associated with them. It considers the role that distance learning methods are likely to play in management education in the future, and makes some comparisons with developments in Canada.

The Spread of Distance Learning in Management Education

The 1980s have seen growing interest in distance learning methods in management education. To some extent this has simply reflected a progressive realisation (that has been occurring in many other fields as well) of the potential of the methods. But it also reflected a gradual awakening of interest in management education—as evidenced, for example, by the steady growth in part-time MBAs from the mid-70s. Recognising this, a number of universities and business schools set about presenting distance taught courses. Henley, the Management College, was the first into the field followed shortly afterwards by the

Open University. Both institutions present a range of modular short courses which build towards a diploma. Henley has also developed an arrangement whereby with additional study, some of it residential, students can obtain a masters degree. The Open University is currently launching its own MBA programme. But in the meantime Strathclyde and Warwick universities (the latter in collaboration with Wolsey Hall, an established correspondence college) have begun presenting their own distance taught MBA programmes, and Durham University and Kingston Polytechnic have also announced their intentions to enter the market.

At the same time, many large companies have begun to use distance learning materials within their own management development programmes.[3] Some are preparing their own materials, others are collaborating with one of the major producers and some are simply choosing the courses that seem most suitable for their purposes. A few private companies have begun to produce and market computer-based training (CBT) and other distance learning materials. Some professional associations (for example, the Chartered Association of Certified Accountants, the Institute of Personnel Management) have either entered the field or extended and up-graded existing correspondence courses. It seems that very similar private sector initiatives have been occurring in Canada.[4]

In the United Kingdom some Industrial Training Boards (for example, for the hotel and catering industry) have also developed programmes. Another major initiative has not been the development, starting in 1984, of a modular distance taught programme by the National Examinations Board for Supervisory Studies (NEBSS). Although the full programme of 47 modules has not been available for long, an impressive 60,000 units have already been sold. This initiative, like many others during the early and mid-eighties, was originally sponsored by the Manpower Services Commission (MSC) which played an absolutely key role in stimulating and financing pilot schemes in open and distance learning in a wide variety of different contexts. More recently, the government's efforts to continue this work have been focused on the Open College which has been pursuing ambitious targets (both financial and in terms of student numbers) for a nationwide system of vocational courses.[5]

The Advantages of Distance Learning

Although state support for these developments has been substantial, the scale of current activity and the continuing growth in demand[6] cannot simply be attributed to supply subsidies and a temporary preoccupation with a fashionable technique. Distance learning methods have become an established element in the management development programmes of many large organizations and the proliferation of suppliers and users continues apace. The National Health Service Training Agency is the latest to embrace the approach.[7] This has happened because distance learning offers demonstrable advantages. Distance learning requires less time away from the job. The modular approach combines selection for relevance with the incentive of a qualification for those interested. It offers an important measure of flexibility in the design of programmes—for example, students can study at their own rather than a group's pace; and it can ensure more cost-effective use of face-to-face course time by ensuring students share a common framework of ideas or techniques. But most important of all, distance learning is seen to work. Well-prepared courses are highly effective and students evaluate them favourably.[8]

Hence, distance learning materials are no longer seen simply as a way of overcoming problems of access (whether due to geography and/or inconvenient timing) that affect face-to-face courses; nor is it simply a matter of being 'cheap and adequate' in relation to large audiences—though both of these classic justifications still apply and remain very important.

Reservations and Problems

Not everyone has been persuaded that distance learning has much to offer in relation to management education. One common suggestion is that distance teaching methods will be perfectly adequate for the 'harder' and knowledge-based aspects of management, but that it will have little to contribute as regards the 'softer', behavioural competencies. Hodgson *et al.* (1987) exemplify this line of thought; they distinguish between a dissemination orientation to education (concerned with the transmission of knowledge) and a developmental orientation (concerned with cultivating independence of mind) and question whether distance learning methods can be an effective medium for the latter.[9] However the suggestion that distance learning cannot be a vehicle for personal development seems to deny the experience of thousands of Open University graduates (Woodley, 1988), quite apart from the fact that students taking Open University management courses regularly highlight the personal development benefits (improved communication skills, greater understanding of self and others, etc.) of courses like The Effective Manager.

A more restricted and considered version of this criticism is based on the argument that group interaction is necessary for the development of a number of key managerial competences. Problem solving in management is simultaneously an intellectual and a social process and managers must learn to consider, challenge and accommodate interpretations very different from their own. Hence programmes that are based on (or include a substantial amount of) group interaction are bound to remain more effective. Such considerations have persuaded some major firms (for example, British Airways) not to use distance learning approaches in management education—even though they use them in other fields (Airey and Goodman, 1986). Clearly, this is a weakness in management education at a distance, but it is one that those involved have been addressing in a number of ways.[10] Moreover, group interaction can still occur, via telephone and computer conferences, even if the participants are not meeting face-to-face. Computer conferencing in particular shows great promise as an educational medium,[11] and it will be particularly appropriate in management education given the advent of E-mail and its derivatives, which are making computer conferencing increasingly common in the management of large organizations. So technology seems to be on the side of distance education and the limitation with respect to the lack of group interaction is likely to become less significant.

Another major question revolves around the issues of cost and quality. As in other fields[12] those preparing management courses were often surprised to discover how much time and effort were needed to prepare quality materials. In consequence, some materials were overpriced and failed to attract a large enough market (for example, the early efforts of the Distance Education Centre at Cranfield Institute of Technology—see Airey and Goodman, 1986), and others were of poor quality.[13] This has posed a harsh dilemma for educational institutions and other providers: on the one hand they saw distance learning advancing rapidly and beginning to pose a competitive threat; on the other hand, to respond by developing their own distance teaching capacity required a very substantial investment whose prospects were highly uncertain in a rapidly changing and increasingly competitive market. Recently, a way out of this dilemma that will be familiar to Canadians has appeared (Konrad and Small, 1986). A consortium of Polytechnics has been formed—under the title, inevitably, of 'The Open Poly'—to collaborate in the preparation and delivery of distance learning materials. If this collaboration is vigorously pursued and adequately resourced by the Polytechnics it could prove a highly significant development. Together, they have the expertise and financial resources to produce quality materials, and the geographical spread both to capture large markets and to provide local support for learners.

A New Challenge: The CMED Proposals

For those of us involved, the developments described have been rapid and exciting. But recently the Council for Management Education and Development (CMED), an industry led body, has put forward a set of proposals—the Management Charter Initiative (MCI)—which, if implemented, would constitute a sea-change in management education in the United Kingdom, and which have enormous implications for distance learning.

The background to this initiative is given, first, by the recognition in industry that a major restructuring of the labour force is underway. In the past a comparatively small proportion of managers controlled large numbers of producers. Increasingly, the trend is towards a comparatively small number of producers and very large numbers of 'knowledge workers' whose activity involves a considerable amount of management (along with their technical or functional specialisms). Hence, many more people must understand and practise management.

The second major impetus was provided by two reports (Handy, 1987; Constable and McCormick, 1987) which painted a disturbing picture of current management training and education in Britain. Most managers receive no formal training and, by comparison with other countries, United Kingdom companies and individual managers invest far less in management development processes. Management educators have not been highly regarded and the only accredited courses that have any status (MBA programmes) vary so widely in content and purpose[14] that, short of scrutinising the syllabus oneself, they provide no reliable indication of what those who have taken them may know or be able to do. However these reports also pointed the way forward emphasising, for example, the complementarity of education and experience in management development, and highlighting advances in management education and training, notably the increasing use of distance learning methods.

The CMED initiative builds on these analyses in the form of an integrated set of proposals aimed at increasing the quality and professionalism of managers through a coherent framework for partnership between individuals, their employers, and educational providers. The main elements are:

- local or sector-based networks of MCI corporate members to share experience and resources, and to identify needs and the most appropriate ways of meeting them.
- a 'common language' for managerial competencies that will assist in specifying the principal needs at the different stages of

an indivdual's career, and the basic standards to be met at different levels of educational provision.

- a nationally recognised, three-tier hierarchical structure of management education based on defined core content and standards; an orientation towards work-based programmes and output assessment; a modular approach allowing vertical and horizontal credit transfer.

- a set of recognised professional qualifications that includes the accreditation of experience.

- a new institution to oversee these arrangements and to represent the parties involved in them.

Of course, ambitious proposals such as these are seldom simply implemented as they stand, nor do they achieve as much as their promoters desire. Nevertheless, it would be a mistake to imagine the MCI will be gradually watered down and in due course forgotten.[15] Leading companies have invested heavily in the initiative, it is strongly supported by government at the highest levels, and a vigorous programme to carry through the proposals is already underway. Quite how, and how far, they can be implemented remains to be seen, but there is a widespread feeling that major changes are unfolding.

Prospects and Implications

So what will be the place of distance learning in this new scheme? The first point to stress is that if the MCI is even moderately successful then the increase in demand for management education and training will be enormous. The elitist, 'high-flyer' connotations will fade; it will be a case of management education, if not for the masses, at least for the mass of middle and junior managers. Not only will companies commit more resources to it but the structure of educational and professional qualifications will provide a substantial incentive for individuals to invest their own time and money in management development.

But as the Constable and McCormick report pointed out, the supply of management educators is limited; hence considerable standardisation and use of distance learning methods becomes essential simply for the supply of reasonable quality programmes to keep pace with demand. If considerations of cost and accessibility are also taken into account, and the fact that funding the development of materials for the new certificate and diploma level qualifications is one way that the government can make things happen, it seems that an explosion in the provision and use of distance learning may be about to take place.

Whether this happens depends partly on the response of the providers of distance learning materials. The MCI proposals present a wide range of challenges to them and to educational institutions in general—for example:

- the need to value experience in management learning and develop new forms of assessment;
- the need to devise ways of sharing control of course design, presentation and accreditation[16] both with other educational providers and with in-company management programmes;
- the need to balance individual and organisational needs, for example, as regards the development of general competences, and those required for a specific job.

It is too soon to say how things are likely to develop, but two very general trends are already clear. First there is likely to be some convergence towards what can be called 'mixed mode' teaching.[17] The distinction between 'distance' and 'face-to-face' methods will become less clearcut, except where for example, geographical isolation is an important factor. The precise mix will vary depending on the subject matter and circumstances, but in general, colleges and companies will both make increasing use of high quality (distance) learning materials in the context of institution based and in-house courses. At the same time, distance learning providers will extend the amount of support and group interaction in their courses, and actively facilitate the addition of face-to-face elements within companies.

Secondly, the 'versioning' of distance taught courses will be come widespread,—indeed, courses will increasingly be designed with this in mind. Distance learning needs large markets to justify the investment required for high quality materials; but the users of management education see quality partly in terms of the direct relevance to a particular type of job or to their industry or company. The way to square this circle is for standard distance taught courses to be 'versioned': either adapted, or topped up with additional materials, or supplemented with face-to-face teaching, in order to meet the requirements of a particular clientele.[18] Again, technology is on the side of this development (text processing and electronic publishing), but it will further complicate the course design process.

Conclusions

The ideas of open and distance learning are changing the face of education and training in the United Kingdom. But their rapid advance is not explained simply by new technologies and the merits of more flexible and accessible learning systems. Increasingly, their progress is tied up with the drive towards a better educated, more skillful workforce, and the advantages they offer for this purpose. Open and distance learning both facilitate and feed on this trend. They have provided an effective cutting edge for change; the desire for economic regeneration and competitiveness has been the engine.

Nowhere is this clearer than in the area of management education. In a number of respects these developments have their parallels in Canada, but the twin trends towards vocationalism and the greater use of distance learning methods are more closely associated in the United Kingdom. Moreover, the recent CMED proposals for a comprehensive restructuring of management education virtually depend on a far wider use of distance learning methods. Hence they will provide a substantial further impetus towards the incorporation of distance learning elements in a wide range of management development programmes.

Notes

1. The common themes are an investment in learning materials and the use of communication technology so that the extent of face-to-face contact between teacher and student in the learning process (and, if need be, between students) can be substantially reduced—and at the limit, substituted for, entirely. The level of investment made, the nature and mix of the materials and technologies used, and the effectiveness of the learning processes vary enormously. See Keegan (1980) or Mugridge and Kaufman (1986) in which Rothe provides an interesting historical perspective.

2. This term is loosely used to refer to programmes which are substantially more accessible to potential learners than traditional, day time, institution-based courses. The barriers to access that open learning programmes attempt to overcome may arise from 'pre-qualifications, age, geographical location, availability, scheduling, learning style and cost' (Cooper, quoted in Fricker, 1986).

3. Distance learning has had obvious attractions for multi-site companies like Shell, British Rail, ICI, the British Steel

Corporation and for major retailers like W.H. Smith, and B. & Q. See Paine ed. (1988) and Airey and Goodman (1986).

4. See Farrel and Haughey (1986) who say (p. 32) 'Private sector initiatives are another major force contributing to the development of open learning systems'; and Seaborne and Zuckernick (1986) who give examples of professional associations using distance learning.

5. See Innes (1988) for an optimistic prospect. Although her plans have had to be cut back by, for example, the closure of the National Distance Learning Centre, the impact on the corporate sector is still likely to be considerable.

6. For example, the Open University is planning on 35 per cent per annum growth in this area.

7. This is through a major collaborative project with the Open University that anticipates 500 hospital and health service managers studying the distance taught version of the course per annum.

8. Rigorous comparative studies would be helpful, but see Lumsden and Scott (1982) for an attempt to compare the learning resulting from a distance taught and a conventionally taught university economics course (the levels of comprehension were similar). Paton and Lay (1986), whose study showed that students on a distance taught management course viewed it more favourably than the conventionally taught courses they had also experienced, is also relevant. This finding is quite striking because it concerned an undergraduate course in management which had not been designed to develop specific skills to the extent that other distance taught management courses have been. Nevertheless, those students with experience of other (face-to-face) courses presented by colleges or through their employers generally considered the distance taught course more useful and relevant. The key factor seems to be the opportunity and requirement to relate course ideas to ones day-to-day experience over an extended period.

9. In the great traditions of social research, this suggestion was an exercise in 'data-free theorising'.

10. For example the Open University School of Management makes this a priority at tutorials and residential schools, and it also takes a number of measures to facilitate the formation of self-help groups among students.

11. This is a medium in which Canada has more experience than the United Kingdom. But see Mason (1988) for current developments at the Open University. Henley is also exploring the possibilities.

12. For example, the training of youth and community workers. See Kitto (1986) for a frank admission of how seriously the time and effort required had been underestimated.

13. The Manpower Services Commission soon recognised that this tendency might discredit the use of distance learning and set about using distance education methods to promote quality in the preparation of distance education materials—see MSC (1988). See also Rumble (1988) for a useful review of the economics of distance education.

14. Some are effectively conversion courses for recent arts or engineering graduates; others concentrate on strategic issues for those with extensive management experience. Some are one year courses; some are two year courses.

15. The idea of management as, in some sense, a profession has attracted the most controversy, but the initiative will still be enormously important even if this element is attenuated.

16. Significantly, the Open University now has a working party on 'The institution as tutor'.

17. Tight (1987) and Lewis (1988) both provide strong arguments why open and distance learning materials and approaches will enter the mainstream of education.

18. Asch and Smith (1988) provide examples from the Open University experience. Henley, the Management College also has extensive experience in this area—see, for an example, Dobson (1988).

References

Airey, F. and M.N. Goodman. 1986. *A Survey of Distance Education in Industry Training*. London: Harbridge House Consulting Group Ltd.

Asch, D. and R. Smith. 1988. 'Management Education: Another Way Forward?'. *Open Learning*, Vol. 3, No.1.

Constable J. and R. McCormick. 1987. *The Making of British Managers*. London: British Institute of Management/ Confederation of British Industry.

Dobson, R. 1988. 'Tomorrow's Training Today.' In Paine ed. (1988).

Farrel G.M. and M. Haughey. 1986. 'The Future of Open Learning.' In Mugridge and Kaufman (1986).

Fricker J. 1986. 'Open Learning: What's in it for Business?' In Paine ed. (1988).

Handy, C. 1987. *The Making of Managers: a Report on Management Education, Training and Development in the USA, West Germany, France, Japan and the UK*. London: NEDO.

Hodgson, V.E., S.J. Mann, and R.S. Snell. 1987. *Beyond Distance Teaching—Towards Open Learning*. Milton Keynes: The Open University Press.

Innes, S. 'The Open College: a Personal View.' In Paine ed. (1988).

Keegan, D. 1980. 'On Defining Distance Education'. *Distance Education*, Vol. 1 No. 1. Queensland, Australia: Darling Downs Institute Press.

Kitto J. 1986. *Holding the Boundaries*. London: YMCA National College.

Konrad, A. and J.M. Small. 1986. 'Consortia in Canadian Distance Education'. In Mugridge and Kaufman (1986).

Lewis, R. 1988. 'Open Learning—The Future.' In Paine ed. (1988).

Lumsden, and A. Scott. 1982. *An output comparison of Open University and Conventional University Students*. Higher Education, Vol. 11, pp. 573-91. The Netherlands: Kluwer Academic Publishers Group.

Manpower Services Commission. 1988. *Ensuring Quality in Open Learning: A Handbook for Action*, Sheffield.

Morgan, R. 1988. 'Computer Conferencing and the University Community'. *Open Learning*, Vol. 3, No. 2. London: Longman.

Mugridge I. and D. Kaufman. 1986. *Distance Education in Canada*. London: Croom Helm.

Paine, N., ed. 1988. *Open Learning in Transition*. Cambridge: National Extension College.

Paton, R. and C. Lay. 1986. 'Learning to Manage and Managing to Learn'. *Open Learning*, Vol. 1, No 3. London: Longman

Rumble G. 1988. 'The Economics of Mass Distance Education'. *Prospects*, Vol. XVIII, No. 1. Paris: Unesco.

Seaborne, K. and A. Zuckernick. 1986. 'Course Design and Development'. In Mugridge and Kaufman (1986).

Tight M. 1987. 'Mixing Distance and Face to Face Higher Education'. *Open Learning*, Vol. 2, No. 1. London: Longman.

Woodley, A. 1988. 'Graduation and Beyond'. *Open Learning*, Vol. 3, No. 1. London: Longman.

Post-Secondary Distance Education: Canada and the United Kingdom Compared

JOHN S. DANIEL
PRESIDENT, LAURENTIAN UNIVERSITY OF SUDBURY

The Origins of Distance Education

History explains why distance education has developed so differently in the post-secondary systems of Canada and the United Kingdom. This history has an unusual twist. Britain often laments that it invents new technologies only to see them adopted with enthusiasm in North America but not at home. For post-secondary distance education it was the other way round. The practice was developed on the frontiers of the Empire, perfected and implemented on a large scale in Britain, and then exported as a mature technology.

The historian Geoffrey Bolton (1986) points out that, until recently, advanced education in England was reserved for the affluent or fortunate and was associated with urban societies. The belief in democratic access to learning which coloured the universities set up in Canada and around the British Empire came from Scotland. The weakening of the assumed link between higher education and city life took place in the pioneering frontier societies themselves. In Bolton's words:

> ...distance education may be seen as one of these innovations which was forged on the frontier of European expansion overseas; ...the history of distance education is to a considerable extent an example of the process by which ideas and techniques developed on the periphery have

> gradually been accepted and absorbed into the old heartland of European culture. (Bolton 1986, 17)

In the pioneering societies primary production was paramount. Once hunters and trappers gave way to agriculturalists the importance of rural interest groups required new approaches to education. Thus at the University of Wisconsin in 1891 teachers in agricultural science (a new discipline) entered into regular correspondence (a new pedagogy) with students who could not attend the campus in Madison. Canada was part of this trend. Queen's University at Kingston began credit correspondence courses in 1889 and in 1907 the University of Saskatchewan began distance education by various methods, including demonstration trains, in subjects such as farming, homemaking and vocational training (Rothe 1986).

Between 1910 and 1940 a number of universities in the British Empire came to offer correspondence courses at a time when there was also growing use of these methods for the education of children. The creation of the International Council for Correspondence Education, at a conference in Victoria, British Columbia in 1938, confirmed the developing role of distance teaching even if it was still regarded as a second-best to instruction on campus or in school.

At this stage, to quote Bolton (1986, 18) again: 'Distance Education was a Cinderella awaiting the Fairy Godmother of improved technology'. She also awaited the right combination of circumstances in higher education for it was two decades after the Second World War before the modern era of post-secondary distance education began. The right combination of circumstances included the decolonisation of the European empires overseas, the pill-induced decline in the birthrate in the Western nations, riots on some campuses in the 1960s, and pressing demands for greater access to universities (if necessary for a second chance as adults) by groups whose attendance at university had been discouraged by social pressures.

The sudden demand for education in newly independent colonies, the fear of a decline in the size of the traditional 18-22 year-old cohort in the West, the harassment of university officials by demonstrating students and increasing attention to social equity combined to make some post-secondary authorities look more closely at distance education. Even though the first universities specialising in distance education had appeared in the 1950s in countries that were not usually considered to be in the vanguard of educational enlightenment, namely the Soviet Union and South Africa, this was an idea whose time had come.

Opening Open Universities

It was in Britain that conditions combined to make possible the establishment of the institution that has been the world's model for post-secondary distance education for the last twenty years: the Open University. Why did this happen in Britain rather than in the countries that had pioneered university distance education?

A book published to mark the 25th anniversary of the National Extension College (Paine 1988) provides several accounts of the social and educational context that led Prime Minister Harold Wilson to call for a 'University of the Air' in a speech in Glasgow in 1963. It also traces the events and influences that moulded this idea into the Open University that began teaching its first 25,000 students in 1971. Of particular interest to this colloquium are the chapters in Paine's book that bring the story up to the present day, describing the creation of the Open College and the attempts by the United Kingdom to weave the strands of distance education and open learning into a better approach to manpower planning.

The planning and launching of the Open University makes a fascinating story that has been well told by its founding vice-chancellor, Walter Perry (1977). He freely admitted that the greatest need for post-secondary distance education in the United Kingdom might well not be for university courses. He was adamant, however, that the first task was to make distance education credible. Harnessing its development to the prestige of university level work was the fastest way to achieve this breakthrough.

What particularly startled overseas observers was the scale on which the Open University was launched. Beginning with a founding class of 25,000 it quickly became the largest university in the United Kingdom—first in student numbers and then in the size of the graduating class. Three factors led the British to this 'big bang' approach. First, the highly restricted entry to conventional universities in the United Kingdom and the almost complete absence of opportunities for part-time university study by working adults provided a huge pool of potential applicants. Second, the commitment to make use of the national radio and TV broadcasting networks of the BBC automatically made the project national in scope. Third, the founding team believed that economics of scale were an advantage of distance education that should be demonstrated to politicians as quickly as possible.

These same factors explain why the pioneers of university distance education in Australia, Canada and the United States could not match the innovative splash made by Britain. In these former colonies participation rates in university study were higher, there was already extensive provision of university programmes to part-time adults and, in any case, populations were much smaller. In North America education is the jurisdiction of the provinces and states. Even the larger of these, such as California, New York and Ontario have only a fraction of Britain's population. Furthermore, the use of national broadcast networks was out of the question in North America. The networks in the United States are essentially commercial. Canada's state networks, the CBC and Radio Canada, are the responsibility of the federal government, which has no constitutional role in Canadian higher education although it pays for it through tax transfers to the provinces. Finally, although educators in North America did not disagree with the claims about economies of scale in distance education, they were not then relevant to their own activities. The jurisdictions were too small to provide tens of thousands of students for a new institution and, in any case, the educational catchwords of the early 1970s were innovation and individualization, not cost-effectiveness.

This is not to say that the launching of the Open University was ignored in Canada. On the contrary, Canadians participated enthusiastically in the worldwide emulation of the initiative that produced some 30 open university projects around the world before the decade of the 1970s was out.

But the Canadians and the British opened their open universities in different ways. In the United Kingdom it was a political decision by the state. The Labour party made the 'University of the Air' a plank in its electoral platform and began nailing it into place when elected. By the time the Open University was ready to open the Tories were back in power and they considered aborting the project. Instead they provided it with relatively massive resources and a direct relationship to government that protected it from the vagaries of the University Grants Commission. The traditional educational establishment thought the idea was madness.

In Canada it happened the other way round. It was the universities themselves which launched the open university projects. Governmental involvement was minimal until British Columbia established the Open Learning Institute in 1978, beginning an active policy interest that has continued to this day in that province. However, in the last decade only the Government of Ontario with its Contact North project for Northern Ontario has joined British Columbia in making distance education a significant element in its post-secondary policy.

Daniel and Smith (1979) have described the genesis of Canada's first open universities, Québec's Télé-université and Alberta's Athabasca University. Both institutions arrived at distance education serendipitously. The Télé-université was launched by the headquarters of the Université de Québec in 1972 in order to add some pedagogical leaven to a network of institutions which had been created with high ideals in 1969 in the aftermath of the upheavals in Berkeley and Paris but was already looking dangerously traditional. Quickly nailing its colours to the mast of distance education, the Télé-université then fought its way to a place in the sun against the consistent opposition of the conventional campuses of the Université de Québec. By 1980 it had around 15,000 students.

Athabasca University was established as an overspill liberal arts campus for the University of Alberta in 1970. However, in 1972 a change in government and a sudden halt in the year-over-year increase in university applications plunged its planning into limbo. The small staff painfully reoriented the project to post-secondary distance education with very little government encouragement until 1978 when a new Order of Council gave the university stability. By then, as at the Télé-université, enrolments had begun to climb and Athabasca has been the fastest-growing university in Canada for much of the past decade.

The present pattern of university distance education in Canada is described comprehensively by Mugridge and Kaufman (1986). In their book, Sweet (1986) divides the providers of distance education at the university level into four categories: correspondence courses (e.g., University of Waterloo); extension and outport programmes (universities such as Brandon, British Columbia, Memorial); open universities (Athabasca, Télé-université and, since 1987, the Open University of the Open Learning Agency of British Columbia); and telecommunications networks (e.g., the Knowledge Network in British Columbia, and Contact North in Ontario).

Such taxonomies are useful but the detailed descriptions of each of these projects presented elsewhere in Mugridge and Kaufman's book show that the boundaries between them are not hard and fast. Ontario's Contact North, the last-mentioned example in the previous paragraph, is indeed a telecommunications network, since it links some 30 learning centres around Northern Ontario by teleconference and computer. But it also has the functions of providing educational counselling in small communities and is closely associated with the extension and correspondence courses of Laurentian University (Roberts, Croft and Derks 1988).

Descriptions of the provision of university distance education in Canada include expressions such as: 'a national potpourri' (Rothe 1986); 'an exciting laboratory of experiments rather than a showroom of finished products' (Daniel 1986); 'statutory permissiveness' (Ellis 1986). They contrast starkly with the terms 'monolithic', 'stand-alone', and 'gigantic' that were once used about the British Open University.

The balkanized nature of university distance education in Canada, with some big projects embedded in conventional universities, even makes it difficult to count the number of students involved. My own guesstimate is that around 100,000 Canadians enrol in university credit courses at a distance each year. This compares to a full-time university enrolment of about 500,000.

Distance Education and Conventional Universities

How do the very different patterns of provision of distance education in Britain and Canada affect the role of distance education in the wider post-secondary systems of the two countries? We shall examine the situation for non-university post-secondary studies in a later section. Here we simply ask what has been the effect of the growth of distance education on the universities as a whole.

One wag remarked that in Britain the chief effect of opening the Open University was to close all the other universities to part-time students even more firmly. Certainly the most striking difference between British and Canadian universities has nothing to do with distance education. It is the almost complete absence of opportunities for British adults to take credit courses on the university campuses in the evening on a part-time basis. The philosophy of equity, access and lifelong learning that motivated the creation of the Open University does not appear to have rubbed off on the rest of the system even though some universities (Strathclyde, Brunel, Warwick) have launched distance education programmes in business studies as a sideline.

The situation is different in Canada because the universities, especially in eastern Canada, are much more accessible to start with. Applications from full-time students for entry to Ontario universities were up 10 per cent this year (on top of 6 per cent last year) yet the government would have regarded it as a crisis if any eligible applicants (those with high school marks of 60 per cent in six subjects) had not been able to find a place somewhere. Then the campus parking lots fill up again in the evening as the part-time students stream into their classes. There is evidence of a slow transfer of part-time students from classroom courses to distance courses for reasons of convenience. It is not always pleasant to turn out on a dark evening in sub-zero temperatures and brush the snow off the car in order to go to university. So a distance course may be preferred even if it normally involves more work.

Big differences in opportunities for part-time students should not, however, hide the common attitude of universities in both countries to one key issue. Both British and Canadian universities flatly refuse to see any role for distance education in the education of the conventional cohort of full-time 18-22 year-olds. In Britain the Open University originally refused applicants under 21 and did research which purported to show that school leavers did not perform well at a distance anyway. Now that several Asian countries are using distance education for very large numbers of 18-22 year olds people in Britain are less categoric about this. In Canada the question does not even arise. A very inexpensive solution to the enrolment pressures in Ontario would have been to organize a few key first year courses by distance education so that students, by taking a mixture of distance and classroom courses, could have attended university full-time without swamping the campus facilities. Instead, of course, all universities asked for more money to build temporary classrooms and mostly got it.

The great virtue of Canada's 'stand-alone' open universities has been to give distance education a status, a quality and a prominence that it would never have achieved through the correspondence and extension programmes of the conventional universities. Sadly, these programmes receive very little institutional attention. Research funding is a much greater priority for university management than accessibility. It will be interesting to see whether Queen's University bothers to celebrate, in 1989, the centenary of its correspondence programme and the beginnings of university distance education in Canada.

Post-Secondary Distance Education at the Non-University Level

Having startled the world 20 years ago by establishing the Open University and provoking a revolution in higher education, Britain surprised the world again by injecting distance education into its manpower training through the creation of the Open College. More recently still the polytechnics have combined to create an Open Poly. The structures of the Open College and the Open Poly are highly decentralised in comparison to the way the Open University is organized.

The aim of the Open College is to bring together broadcasters, educationalists and industry 'to provide vocational education and training for a mass audience ... using open learning to widen access to training' (Innes 1988). Unlike the Open University which operates its own regional network, for the Open University 'local support is provided by colleges, employers and other learning establishments in both the public and private sectors'.

It would be wrong, however, to present the Open College as a brand-new initiative. It is the successor to a number of schemes of Britain's Training Agency (formerly the Manpower Services Commission) which had implemented the five-year Open Tech programme from 1982-87 and runs the Youth Training Scheme. The United Kingdom's continuous succession of training bodies and projects has been difficult enough to follow for the British themselves, let alone for foreigners. However, as a result of this consistent government interest open learning has come to play a significant role in education and training in the United Kingdom (Temple 1988). So much so that the approaches of open learning and distance education have now been absorbed into the bloodstream of many institutions (Rowlands 1988).

In Canada there has been less progress. Distance education is in its infancy in the country's college system—which is not really a system since every province defines its colleges differently. In an article on distance education programmes in community colleges Dennison (1986) found he had to spend half the paper describing the college system before summarizing the colleges' distance education activities. He concludes that 'colleges have failed to accommodate a segment of the community who cannot, or prefer not to, use face-to-face instruction... open learning constitutes a challenge which cannot be ignored'.

Of considerable importance to the colleges as they face this challenge is the attitude of the federal government which, through the Department of Employment and Immigration Canada, is the paymaster for much of their work. There are signs that the department is increasingly aware of the potential for open learning in training.

International Initiatives

Another instance of Canada's commitment to distance education is the role it has taken in recent international initiatives. In September 1987 Canada hosted the summit of francophone countries and was a catalyst for the creation of the Centre International Francophone pour la Formation à Distance (CIFFAD), which is now based in Montreal. In October 1987, when the biennial meeting of the heads of Commonwealth governments was held in Vancouver, Canada and Britain supported the planning of a cooperative venture in distance education which has since been launched as The Commonwealth of Learning. Based in Vancouver, it is the first Commonwealth organization to have its headquarters away from London. It is also the first multi-lateral Commonwealth project to which developing countries (Brunei Darussalam, India, Nigeria) have made significant contributions in convertible currency.

Conclusion

Inspired by the results of the British government's decision to create the Open University, Canadian institutions, with little government involvement, have developed a diversity of university distance education programmes that serve about 100,000 students. Canada will likely also follow the British lead in applying distance education to vocational and manpower training, although this application will require more involvement by Canadian governments.

References

Bolton, G. 1986. The Opportunities of Distance. In *Flexible Designs for Learning*, International Council for Distance Education, pp. 13-23.

Commonwealth Secretariat. 1987. Commonwealth Heads of Government Meeting Vancouver 1987, Record of Session Six.

Daniel, J.S. 1986. 'Preface'. In *Distance Education in Canada*, ed. by I. Mugridge and D. Kaufman. Croom Helm, p. iii.

Daniel, J.S. and W.A.S. Smith. 1979. 'Opening Open Universities: The Canadian Experience'. *Canadian Journal of Higher Education*, IX-2, pp. 63-74.

Dennison, J. 1986. 'Community Colleges'. In *Distance Education in Canada*, ed. by I. Mugridge and D. Kaufman. Croom Helm, pp. 185-193.

Ellis, J.F. 1986. 'Government Policies'. In *Distance Education in Canada*, ed. by I. Mugridge and D. Kaufman. Croom Helm, pp. 25-29.

Innes, S. 1988. 'The Open College: A Personal View'. In *Open Learning in Transition—An Agenda for Action*, ed. by N. Paine. National Extension College, pp. 233-245.

Mugridge, I. and D. Kaufman, eds. 1986. *Distance Education in Canada*. Croom Helm.

Paine, N., ed. 1988. *Open Learning in Transition: An Agenda for Action*, National Extension College.

Perry, W. 1977. *The Open University*. San Francisco: Jossey-Bass.

Roberts, J., M. Croft and P. Derks. 1988. 'Contact North/Contact Nord: A model for distance education project administration'. In *Developing Distance Education*, ed. by D. Sewart and J.S. Daniel. Oslo: International Council for Distance Education, pp. 388-390.

Rothe, J.P. 1986. 'An Historical Perspective'. In I. Mugridge and D. Kaufman, op. cit., pp. 4-24.

Rowlands, N. 1988. 'Current developments at Central Manchester College'. In N. Paine, op. cit., pp. 274-290.

Sweet, R. 1986. 'University Programmes'. In I. Mugridge and D. Kaufman, op. cit., pp. 169-184.

Temple, H. 1988. 'Open Learning in a Changing Climate'. In N. Paine, op. cit., pp. 201-211.

V
PRIVATE SECTOR PARTICIPATION

An Example of Successful School/Industry Links: The East London Compact

J.F. JARVIS, REGIONAL COMMUNITY AFFAIRS DIRECTOR
  WHITBREAD & COMPANY
  MANAGER, EAST LONDON COMPACT

Introduction

On the 7th March 1988, the Prime Minister of Great Britain launched the Government's Inner City Programme 'Action for Cities'. One of the few new initiatives in this announcement was the Department of Employment plan to give development funding and further support to Education Business Compacts in urban programme areas of the United Kingdom. Subsequently, in August, the Secretary of State for Employment, the Right Honourable Norman Fowler, MP, announced support for 30 Compacts.

Why a Partnership and Compact

The need for action to improve education standards in London schools had clearly been identified by the Inner London Education Authority and the London Enterprise Agency and subsequently nationally by the Government. There was a lack of motivation amongst school pupils and teachers caused by the 'Why bother?' attitude, 'there are no opportunities for us in the London business'. This in turn has led to low academic results and an unacceptable level of truancy. Together with the skill mismatch that now exists, this had lead to the formation of education-business partnerships throughout the United Kingdom dedicated to developing schemes for improving education standards.

The first of these was the London Education Business Partnership, from which the East London Compact was born.

Formation of the London Education Business Partnership (LEBP)

To understand a Compact and to learn how it initially came to the United Kingdom, it is necessary to go back to 1984 and the formation of the London Education Business Partnership (LEBP). In that year, members of the Board of the London Enterprise Agency (LEntA) visited New York and learned about the New York City Partnership and its successful links with the city's Education Department.

As a result of this visit, the LEBP was formed. A true partnership between the Inter London Education Authority (ILEA) and London business, as represented by the LEntA membership.

The Inner London Education Authority provides education for a lifetime within its 1,091 schools, colleges, youth centres and adult facilities. Londoners aged from under five to over fifty benefit from one of the world's most comprehensive education service. It encompasses an area of 114 square miles of London with a school population of over 400,000 students and 26,000 teachers. Within these figures there are 146 secondary schools with a total of nearly 120,000 students.

LEntA was set up to enable the nation's major companies to work together to tackle some of the problems of London's Inner City. LEntA is backed by 17 major companies who provide funding, secondees and other forms of goodwill and, since 1986, has become a company limited by guarantee.

It's primary objectives are:

– To create viable jobs and economic growth through expansion of small businesses in the capital.
– To enable the private sector, either independently or in partnership with the public sector, to tackle specific projects which aid inner city regeneration.
– Where appropriate, to undertake innovative projects which can either be applied in other parts of the United Kingdom or have an overall national benefit.

The London Education Business Partnership quickly developed its aims which were:

– To increase involvement and understanding between the Authority and business.
– To support curriculum change giving more emphasis to the development of personal skills and qualities.

- To help develop a 'record of achievement' for every pupil to show personal qualities as well as examination results.
- To help overcome discrimination against ethnic minorities.
- To support wider career opportunities for girls.
- To foster exchange schemes between teachers and business.
- To support research projects related to these aims.
- To develop enterprise.

The LEntA Trust was formed to raise funds for partnership ctivities. A council was formed with two members from each of the trustees: LEntA, TUC and the ILEA. This was supported by an executive, that now has a full time chief executive to whom Compact directors report.

London Education Business Partnership—Initial Activities

It was at the time of the formation of the Partnership that the Inner London Education Authority published its report on 'Improving Secondary Schools' in which it highlighted 'four aspects' of achievement that should be recognised in any school leaver:
- The ability to retain knowledge—the only skill assessed by examination.
- The ability to use information.
- Interpersonal skills.
- Motivation.

The Education Minister at the time, Sir Keith Joseph had suggested that employers wanted all these qualities, and yet only recognised the first when selecting for interview. He accused employers of giving teachers a scrambled message, saying that they wanted a well rounded, capable recruit, but advertised for candidates with O' or A' levels.

This gave rise to the Partnership's first task, the development of the London Record of Achievement which will record the whole range of a school leaver's activities and interest, not just examination results: in other words, a pupil's profile. An ILEA Team worked together with an employers group, lead by the, personnel director of UB Restaurants to develop this record which is now being piloted in 20 ILEA schools.

However, whilst both the London Record of Achievement and the other Partnership activities were beginning to break down the misunderstanding between education and employers, it was not really addressing the main Partnership aim—to improve education standards in the ILEA Schools.

It was in September 1986, only just over two years ago, that a team from the LEBP, together with the ILEA's chief education officer visited Boston, Massachusetts to attend the Business in the Community Conference on 'Youth at Work'. This conference was chaired by the Prince of Wales and naturally included a 'look at' the Boston Compact. They recognised a number of similarities with the education problems in Boston and East London. The Boston Compact appeared to have some of the answers, so on their return to the United Kingdom it was agreed that a feasibility study be carried out.

East London Compact (Feasibility Study)

The Feasibility Study Group first met on 7 October 1987. It consisted of three head teachers, three ILEA officers, the principal careers officer and six business representatives. Its task was 'to assess whether it was possible to devise and implement an agreement between existing and potential employers in Docklands and schools and colleges in Tower Hamlets and Hackney, which could lead to priority hiring of local school and college leavers and improvement in the education achievement and the motivation of young people'.

The area of Tower Hamlets and Hackney was rated amongst the worst of the deprived inner cities, it had a high level of unemployment amongst school leavers, involving a wide variety of ethnic groups. there existed some religious and community prejudices with evidence of racial tension and conflict. Contrary to patterns elsewhere, the school rolls were expected to increase. There was evidence from existing employers in Docklands and surrounding areas of high turnover (wastage) and a shortage of potential employees. In general employers seem prepared to recruit from the local schools providing the school leaver standards meet their selection criteria.

The study therefore recommended in December 1986 that a pilot scheme be run in Hackney and Tower Hamlets.

East London Compact Pilot Phase

Following the recommendation of the feasibility study, Whitbread & Co Plc seconded a senior manager in January 1987 to be the first Compact director with the objective of developing the pilot phase.

ILEA identified four schools, which quickly increased to six in Hackney and Tower Hamlets. The first task was to agree measurable goals for both pupils and schools. The school heads together with officers from the ILEA worked with the Compact director to identify relevant goals that in the end have proved to be more extensive than those used in Boston.

The school and pupil goals were:

Activity	School Goals Over the Course of Each Academic Year
ATTENDANCE (based on 10 sessions per week)	An average annual attendance rate of not less than 80% of fourth and fifth year students or, alternatively, an improvement of 5% on previous year.
PUNCTUALITY	An average annual rate of not less than 90% for punctuality at registration for fourth and fifth year students.
COMPLETION OF SELECTED COURSES	An average course completion rate of not less than 80% or, alternatively, an improvement of 5% in the previous year's figures.
ASSESSMENT OF FOUR ASPECTS OF ACHIEVEMENT	The curriculum should enable students to develop competencies in the four aspects of achievement: 1. The acquisition and use of information. 2. The practical application of knowledge. 3. Personal and social skills, including communication skills. 4. Motivation, commitment and enterprise.
CERTIFICATION AND QUALIFICATION	Every course in the fourth and fifth years should have some appropriate certification; for example:
WORK EXPERIENCE	Two weeks, work experience as part of the curriculum offer should be provided.
CONTINUING EDUCATION	THE INTENTION OF THE COMPACT IS TO IMPROVE PARTICIPATION IN CONTINUING EDUCATION IN EITHER SCHOOLS OR COLLEGES
PREPARATION FOR ADULT LIFE	Each school should provide for: 1. Meetings with the parents of fourth and fifth year students. 2. Careers guidance. 3. Links with and service to the local community. 4. Links with employers.

Activity	Personal Goals For Fourth and Fifth Year Students
ATTENDANCE (based on 10 sessions per week)	Not less than 85% attendance at morning and afternoon sessions for each of fourth and fifth years.
PUNCTUALITY	Not less than 90% punctuality at morning and afternoon registration for each of fourth and fifth years.
COMPLETION OF SELECTED COURSES	Satisfactory completion of the two year course in the 4/5th years. Completion involves meeting no less than 90% of deadlines for all assignments, including homework.
ASSESSMENT OF FOUR ASPECTS OF ACHIEVEMENT	Completing the London Record of Achievement or a record of development relating to the four aspects of achievement.
CERTIFICATION AND QUALIFICATION	Providing evidence of certification or credits gained, including a graded result in a recognised examination in English, or English as a second language and mathematics.
WORK EXPERIENCE	Satisfactory completion of two weeks' work experience.
CONTINUING EDUCATION	THE INTENTION OF THE COMPACT IS TO IMPROVE PARTICIPATION IN CONTINUING EDUCATION IN EITHER SCHOOLS OR COLLEGES
PREPARATION FOR ADULT LIFE	Satisfactory attendance in a full personal social and health education course. This will include careers guidance and participation in a community service project and evidence of developing self-respect and respect for others.

The essence of the Compact is a true partnership between education and employers, supported by a clear understanding between the partners to achieve their aims. It was therefore found necessary to also have measurable goals for the employers.

A small team of employers, under the chairmanship of the personnel director of John Laing Construction Ltd., who had been on the visit to Boston, worked with the Compact director to develop their goals.

These were:

1. To give priority in offers for employment to all students from the schools taking part in this pilot project who have achieved their personal goals.

2. To offer the resources of the business sector at all levels to support the development of links between schools and industry in all aspects of the curriculum.

3. To co-operate with schools over requests;
   a) For work experience, work shadowing and holiday jobs, for pupils.
   b) For secondments of teachers to industry.
   c) To release business people to shadow teachers.

4. To ensure an equal opportunities approach in considering school-leavers for employment.

5. To interview all students with special needs from the school taking part, in order to find, with the aid of the Careers Services, suitable opportunities for them.

6. To provide, in co-operation with ILEA Careers Service and Careers Teachers from the participating schools, a counselling service for those who, after three interviews, have not obtained a job.

7. To provide permanent jobs.

8. To ensure each offer of employment includes access to a recognised company training programme which:
   a) provides adequate induction for new recruits.
   b) provides regular counselling during the first year of employment.
   c) is properly structured and controlled and includes the opportunity for part-time day release where appropriate.
   d) encourages recruits to continue their studies.
   e) provides access to facilities through which further qualifications can be achieved.

Having identified and agreed the goals for both parties, it was necessary to specify the client groups. As far as the schools were concerned, the Careers Service was able to state that there were 500 potential 16 year-old school leavers in July 1988, that is, at the end of the first academic year of the Compact. However, woo of these would either stay on in education, go to jobs without any outside help or stay at home, leaving some 300 pupils who could benefit from the Compact.

With this in mind it was necessary to recruit sufficient employers who could give jobs to the 300 pupils, jobs with training and development, and which were within an easy travel to work area from the pupil's homes. Initially recruitment was targeted in the fast growing Docklands area, but due to development delays, opportunities were sought further afield. Recruitment was targeted at 50 employers. The stage was now set, and the Prince of Wales formally launched the East London Compact at a large gathering of interested employers at Mulberry School (a girl's school with 85 per cent Bangladeshi pupils) on September 16th, 1987.

Following the launch, a programme of meetings, briefings and discussion groups were held in the schools to inform pupils, staff and parents of the Compact aims. Schools developed their own activities to both encourage and monitor progress towards the goals. A programme of visits to the schools by potential employers helped significantly to break down the artificial barriers that existed. Schools realised there were opportunities for 'Inner City pupils' in business and business recognised the potential of these pupils. Presentations were made to the employers groups and to individual business people to encourage them to join the Compact and offer job opportunities to successful pupils. To-date nearly 50 employers have signed a letter of intent.

As the pilot scheme grew it was considered that some formal management structure should be developed administer, monitor tand coordinate the various joint activities. It should incorporate existing structures and not create a further bureaucracy.

East London Compact Management Structure

The committees and structures that have been developed are:

    a) *Employers Group*—quarterly meetings

        To co-ordinate and develop employers' response to goals; to include representatives from each business sector in the area chaired by a senior businessman. Compact director to attend.

b) *Schools/College Heads/Principals Group*—termly meetings

To co-ordinate and develop schools response to goals; to include heads/principals of all schools/colleges in Compacts chaired by one of the heads/principals. Compact director to attend.

c) *School/College Committee*—monthly meetings

To ensure Compact Goals are achieved within schools. To plan, manage and evaluate Compact activities. To include heads of 4th and 5th years, Careers teacher, Careers officer, LRA Development officer and Divisional Industry Schools Co-ordinator (DISCO).

d) *Project Leaders Committee*—monthly meetings

To develop and manage joint school/business activities. To include Careers Service representative, Work Experience co-ordinator, Teacher Secondment co-ordinator, TWL co-ordinator, Business representative, LEBP Schools Project director, London Record of Achievement representative, Research & Statistics etc. Compact Director to chair.

The roles are thus:

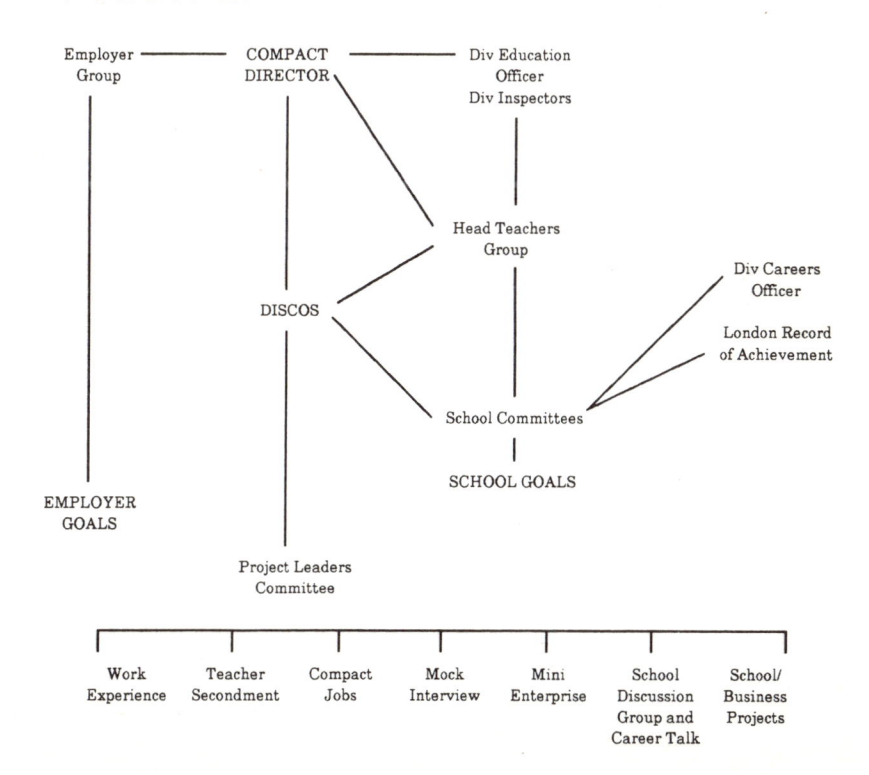

Working with the Compact director is a small team of project leaders who are full or part-time secondees with specific tasks to carry out. They are:

- a work experience co-ordinator.
- a supply teacher to stand in for teachers on work experience.
- a Careers Service officer.
- the Divisional Industry Schools co-ordinator.
- employers managing specific tasks such as mock interviews, mini-enterprises, careers tasks and discussion groups.
- transition to Working Life co-ordinator.
- London Record of Achievement co-ordinator.

Funding

Currently the East London Compact is totally funded by the private sector with money raised from the LEntA Trust. Its main costs are staff. At present the Compact director is on secondment, and is provided with an office, together with support facilities by his firm, but his assistant must be paid for. The ILEA have seconded 4 staff almost full time, but with the state of their budget it is unlikely that this can continue for much longer. Additional sources of funding will have to be found. If everything had to be paid for, it is estimated that a Compact the size of the East London pilot could cost £150,000 per annum (1987).

Success 1988

At the time of writing it is too early to measure the rate of success with any great accuracy, but there are some very clear indicators.

- School attendance has increased by 8 per cent in the fourth year and 5 per cent in the fifth year.
- It has been reported from a number of schools that there is likely to be at least double the staying-on rate.
- Over 40 employers have signed the 'Letter of Intent' ranging from small shop keepers prepared to take one pupil, to large national organisations prepared to take up to 30 pupils.
- Over 40 teachers have had a week secondment to business.
- 60 pupils have experienced mock interviews with employers.

- Over 100 representatives from employers have visited the six schools, taking part in discussion groups, careers talks and even shadowing teachers.
- Parents are beginning to look for 'Compact' schools for their children, this is noticeable amongst the Bangladeshi community.

Bearing in mind the short life of the Compact, there are three of these successes that have had the greatest effect:

1. Visits by employers to the schools have done more to break down the anticipated and unrealistic barriers between schools and employers than any other single activity. There have been suspicions from both sides: the pupils' view that rich and selfish employers wanted to control education for their own ends; and the employers' view that pupils from schools in these deprived areas were unemployable. The contrary is in fact the case and many links between the two sides have been developed.
2. Teachers' secondment to business has helped the teaching of the world of work considerably. Teachers have experienced the entry jobs that a 16 year-old would be offered; they have learned how people are trained, developed and appraised in the commercial world, how people work together in teams, and how problems are solved and decisions made. Links have been developed with specific functions and school subjects that have brought real-life projects into the classroom.
3. Work experience for pupils has probably had the greatest influence on the desire to continue in education. Some may say that continuing in education is an easy option, but the majority recognise now that there are opportunities for them in the business world, that the people they have met are quite ordinary friendly people just like themselves, and that they can do well if they upgrade their educational standards.

Lessons Learned from the Pilot

Although in general the pilot is rated as very successful, there are some specific areas of improvement necessary.

- School selection should be made on a more specific criteria, based on the schools ability to deliver the goals.
- More time should be spent on briefing school staff, particularly the junior grades as well as pupils and parents.

- Time must be found in school staff time-tables to enable them to work more effectively on the Compact.

- Briefing, debriefing and monitoring of all parties for both teacher secondments and work experience placements should be improved considerably.

- Management within the schools as well as across the schools of Compact work should be improved.

- There should be closer co-ordination between the work of Careers Teachers and Careers Service with a general upgrading of this whole areas.

- As the Compact grows in size, it will be necessary to develop a computer data base for both work experience and job appointments. These two activities together with teacher secondments when operated throughout the whole of London could produce an enormous logistical problem that only an up-to-date information system could handle. It is necessary to schedule these placements evenly across the year. At present they are made in blocks to suit the academic year, but blocks of such a size that employers cannot absorb them.

- The school goals are currently being revised. There is criticism that some overlap, they are inflexible and motivate too narrow a band of pupils. They may not always be appropriate and are open to misinterpretation.

- The recruitment of employers has proved to be one of the hardest activities. It has been necessary for them to reconsider the relevance of their recruitment and selection procedures as well as their training programmes. An employed status YTS programme is considered to be the minimum training an employer should provide.

The Future

As a result of East London Compact receiving a lot of good publicity, other education authorities throughout the country are considering ways of developing Compacts that suit their own particular environment. This initiative was given a tremendous boost by the decision of the Training Commission to give development funding to 30 potential Compacts.

Currently the East London Compact is growing from six schools to 10 schools and from 50 employers to 100 employers. London itself will have four Compacts under the umbrella of the London Education

Business Partnership: North London with a director seconded from J. Sainsbury, West London with a director seconded by Marks & Spencer Plc, South East London with a director seconded by Citibank and East London with a director seconded by Whitbread & Co Plc.

Why Employers Should be Involved

There are three important commercial reasons for employers' commitment to Compacts:

1. The serious reduction in school leavers projected for the early 1990s—something like 20 per cent. There will be job opportunities for every school leaver, but as technology develops so must the skills of those that will use it, otherwise they will remain unemployable.

2. The need for stable, healthy and attractive inner cities in which employees can work and enjoy their leisure peacefully and the business can trade successfully.

3. The mobility of labour within the EEC in 1992 which will create more competition for jobs and therefore create a need for better standards of education in the United Kingdom.

Training and Development: The Shadow Higher Education System in Canada

GILLES PAQUET
FACULTY OF ADMINISTRATION, UNIVERSITY OF OTTAWA*

> Les vrais événements nous échappent... les Parisiens de 1815 riaient de voir sur la Seine un bateau à vapeur, affreuse machine qu'ils pensaient éphémère.
>
> — Alexandre Vialatte

Introduction

The traditional higher education enterprise has blossomed in Canada over the last quarter of a century. Post-secondary full-time enrolment grew more than five-fold between the early 1960s and the mid 1980s; the annual cost of the enterprise has grown to some $9.3 billions in the mid-1980s (National Forum 1987). The performance of the traditional post-secondary enterprise (PSE) has been impressive in terms of accessibility: more than 50 per cent of high school graduates now proceed directly to a post-secondary institution (Leblanc 1987).

Yet the Canadian PSE faces a sort of crisis of confidence. An array of critics have complained: (1) that the government share of the operating expenditures of the PSE is too high (78 per cent); (2) that the standards of the PSE are too low, and consequently the quality of the output is inadequate; (3) that the PSE caters only to the richer students (accessibility); (4) that it provides an education that is not

---

* This work was done while the author was Scholar-in-Residence at the Institute for Research on Public Policy. The help of the Institute is gratefully acknowledged. The analysis, results, and opinions contained in this paper do not necessarily reflect the views of the Institute. The usual caveat applies.

The assistance of Anne Burgess, Georges Gauthier, Jeff Greenberg, Marc Racette and Diane Séguin and the comments of Ainslie Clark and Christian Navarre are gratefully acknowledged.

called for by the market place (relevance); and (5) that it is not optimally managed (waste) (Paquet/von Zur Muehlen 1988).

The purpose of this paper is to look at some aspects of item (4) in the above list. Employers have expressed dissatisfaction with graduates from the PSE: some have simply echoed their complaints to task forces and committees (e.g., Conseil de la Science et de la Technologie du Québec 1985); other employers have developed some alternative post-secondary education of their own for their employees, or secured access to such alternatives from non-conventional providers. For the *learning enterprise* is not restricted to the traditional PSE: private employers have developed in-house courses and programmes, government agencies have created in-house programmes and schools, and both private and public concerns have bought formal courses and programmes from private firms in the education business providing such services. According to some estimates, these formal non-traditional activities have grown considerably over the last decade or two and might now amount to expenditures of the order of $2 to $3 billions per year in Canada (Reeves 1983).

To some, this growth of private production of higher education is clear evidence that the post-secondary education produced by the traditional providers is found wanting, that it is not what the market wants. To others, the new type of post-secondary education is in fact not education at all, but training and development, a complement, not a substitute for standard post-secondary education (Lynton 1984: Ch.6). This sort of partitioning (education *versus* training and personal development) may be regarded as a somewhat spurious and unclear delineation in practice (Nash/Hawthorne 1987) but it remains in good currency, especially in traditional institutions. Yet the growing overlap of courses and seminars offered in the different categories and the increasing importance of formal recognition and accreditation of employer-sponsored instruction would appear to indicate that there is a continuum from education to training and development.

In the next section, a TED (training, education, development) problématique is sketched; in section 3, a few guesstimates are suggested of the size, shape and nature of non-traditional higher education services, and some trends and drifts in the evolution of this shadow higher education system are noted; section 4 explores alternative strategies open to governments and to traditional post-secondary institutions in Canada. The conclusion attempts to ascertain the direction in which the Canadian learning enterprise is most likely to evolve.

Problématique

Education, broadly speaking, is defined as being concerned with the development of the mind and the ability to reason; training as pertaining to skill development; personal development as broadly embracing components of both, but also development of character, self-awareness and interpersonal/communication capabilities and competence (Peterfreund 1976).

Educators, trainers and developers defend different strategies. For educators, operating in the Rousseau-Dewey tradition, the shaping of the mind and the ability to reason is somewhat content-neutral and focused on general principles, on general knowledge, for this is the way to learn how to think critically. For trainers, knowledge is skill and skill is knowledge, and there is no way to develop general abilities without focusing on procedural and substantive schemata that are highly specific to the task at hand. For developers, the cornerstone might be loosely called an anthropological theory of education: knowledge and skills can be developed only on the basis of a capacity to grow as a human being within a human community to which one is acculturated (Hirsch 1988).

These three notions are ideal-types in most discussions, but much of what is done under any of these labels turns out to have educational, training and developmental components. Any curriculum, course or seminar is a mix of these three components and may be represented as located somewhere within a triangle of human capital formation where each apex is an ideal-typical representation of education, training and personal development.

Figure 1
The Human Capital Formation Triangle

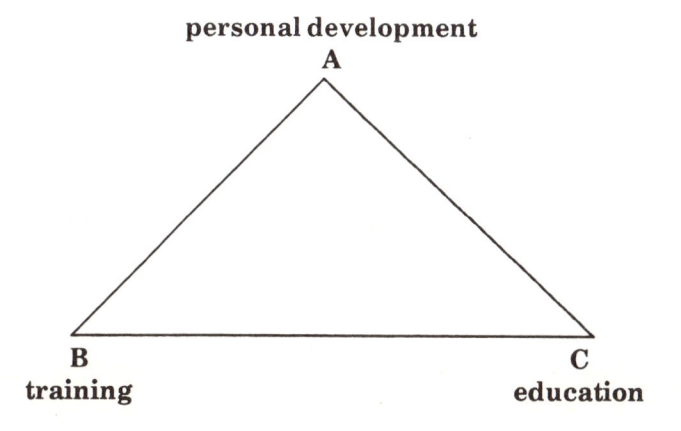

The center of gravity of the traditional Canadian PSE—and of any other national system for that matter—should be mappable as a point or as a zone within this triangle. Some national strategies may have privileged one component or another; all have evolved through time, and their drift should be traceable within the triangle. Indeed, any PSE enterprise—ideally—should, through a diversity of institutions, cater to the diversity of private demands and public needs. Grosso modo, one might stylize the strategies proposed by educators, trainers and developers by saying that educators bet predominantly on C as the baseline, trainers on B, and developers on A.

In the 19th and early 20th centuries, the mix of education, training and development in traditional post-secondary education in Canada was probably more balanced than it is now. Much importance was given to each component of human capital formation, through a diversity of institutions and arrangements. During the first half of the 20th century, however, a formal philosophy of education, inspired by Jean-Jacques Rousseau and John Dewey and putting the emphasis on education as a formal process of shaping of mind and reason that could be effected through content-neutral curricula, came into good currency. Education, as apex C, became the lynch-pin of the PSE. This philosophy took hold in the United States, but filtered to Canada. Segments of the PSE became more specialised, and a division of labour crystallised more sharply between the different institutions— universities, colleges, technical schools etc.—some with a higher or a lower status according to the mix of these components they provided.

The positivist revolution, together with the Rousseau-Dewey tradition, shifted the center of gravity of the PSE by imposing a certain formalism on the post-secondary enterprise: there was more and more emphasis on theory, general principles and the scientific method, and less and less on matters pertaining to the 'oral', the 'particular', the 'local' and the 'timely' (Toulmin 1988). What has evolved in universities is a curriculum made up of a variety of general principles and broad surveys, providing the necessary elements for the educated person to think critically. The idea of a true vocationally-oriented higher education system disappeared (Gunderson 1978) and the ruling philosophy of education percolated down to the secondary level where the skill component dwindled, and general content-free curricula prospered (Adams 1980).

It is true that technical schools, colleges and polytechnics developed a different brand of curriculum—more practical and more training-intensive—but the social status of these programmes remained relatively low, and the training they purported to give became more and more 'tainted' by the ruling educational philosophy. A recent report of the Canadian Chamber of Commerce was quite harsh in evaluating these institutions: the students are being trained on outdated equipment, and the quality of instruction is so low that 'students graduate without sufficient skills or ability to pursue their chosen careers effectively' (Basken et al. 1988).

The Rousseau-Dewey ruling philosophy of education has been challenged by recent work on cognition. Critical thinking, it would appear, evolves not from general content-free principles or methodologies, but from schemata that are highly specific to the task at hand. The learning enterprise is meant to ensure that one acquires a fair number of such schemata, shared by others in the community, so as to be able to communicate competently and effectively with them—providing the person with a sort of 'cultural currency' in the sense that economists give to existing national currencies (Hirsch 1988). The development of this basic currency—capacious and vague, but fundamental to communicative competence and competitiveness—cannot be produced either through general disembodied principles, in the manner of the traditional curricula, or simply through skill-building, in the manner one proceeds to coach an athlete to success. 'Facts and skills are inseparable' and background knowledge—even that which is specific culturally and nationally—is of great import in the development of critical reason, but also in personal growth as a competent citizen (Paquet 1989).

Some Guesstimates, Trends and Drifts

The new practical philosophy of education has not yet translated into the practices of the mainstream of the traditional PSE: over the last twenty years, there has been a drift toward a yet higher degree of technical sophistication that has reduced significantly both the personal development component and the real usable skill content of education.

This drift away from training and development in the traditional PSE has triggered a reaction in the rest of the learning enterprise. Firms and individuals have had to take on an important training and development function, for high school graduates and general degree holders have been 'unskilled' as they entered the labour market (Adams 1980). It has not been necessary to develop formal programmes, but some training and development in the firm or on one's own has become essential in this context.

The process has not evolved as rapidly in Canada as it has in the United States, for a variety of reasons: given the fabric of our resource-based economy, the centrality of knowledge and training in economic growth has not always been sufficiently recognised; as a result, the industrial training system in place is weak in Canada, despite the large sums spent on training by the Canadian government (Adams 1980). Other reasons for this underdevelopment have to do with both the size of the average Canadian firm and the high degree of foreign control of the Canadian economy: small firms rely much more heavily on informal training (not recorded and difficult to evaluate) and, *ceteris paribus* foreign-controlled firms are less likely to spend resources locally on national trainees, for they often have training facilities abroad. Indeed these facilities are often degree-granting institutions (Eurich 1985; Wilcox 1987).

Any measurement of this ill-understood activity is made difficult by the many definitions of training and development activities in use. Using rather broad definitions, the Economic Council of Canada comes up with establishment training rates that are that three times as large as those proposed by Statistics Canada with its much narrower definition (Adams 1980). Even though Table 1 contains only rough guesstimates, these numbers show that the sums spent by the traditional providers (universities and colleges) represent only one third of the learning enterprise at the post-secondary level, and that the great bulk of non-traditional learning is done through informal arrangements (Adams 1980). Moreover, detailed analyses of the Canadian learning enterprise have revealed that Canada lags behind several European countries (Labour Canada 1979).

a. *Demand for Formal Non-traditional PSE Services*

Employment and Immigration Canada surveyed 7652 firms in 1983-84 on their official/formal training activities (Employment and Immigration 1988). The comparability with data from either the Economic Council of Canada (Human Resources Survey 1979) or from Statistics Canada or from ad hoc commissions of inquiry (Commission on Educational Leave and Productivity 1979) is at best problematic, but a number of conclusions are clear: (1) the percentage of establishments with a training plan has increased, (2) the training rate has grown particularly rapidly in manufacturing, trade and services, (3) the average length of employer-sponsored training has increased, and (4) the training rate remains—as had been noted in earlier surveys—much lower for Quebec establishments surveyed than for establishments in the rest of Canada. It is clear that the training rate for the economy as a whole has increased substantially over the last decade.

The public sector was not surveyed in 1983-84, but it is well-known that it has a higher than average percentage of establishments with training plans. In that sense, the public sector is closer in behaviour to large private firms.

Table 1
A View of the Structure of the Learning Enterprise
(in billions of Canada dollars)

	United States	Canada
Traditional PSE	$ 94.0	$ 9.3[1]
Employee informal training	180.0	18.0[2]
Employee formal training	30.0	2.0[3]
Government training	5.0	1.0[4]

Source: United States: (Carnavale 1986)
Canada: (1) Statistics Canada
(2) Canadian value is assumed to be 10% of the U.S. total
(3) minimum amount suggested by (Reeves 1983)
(4) rough aggregation of major components (government training centres, in-house training, manpower training policy, etc.,) confirmed by the fact that the Canadian government expenditures on training per labour force members are approximatively twice that of the United States (Gunderson 1978).

Our conjecture about the Canadian scene is reinforced by a recent study of the US scene. This study shows a sharp acceleration of training and development programmes in large US companies in response to heightened global competition and to new skills and knowledge needs: 'companies are strengthening and widening the role of corporate training departments' (Lusterman 1985). Our own informal discussions with a number persons responsible for training and development in Canadian companies would appear to confirm that in Canada as well training and development has become a 'key strategic tool' (Olson 1986).

b. *Supply of Formal Non-traditional PSE Services*

In the United States, it has been suggested that approximately 4000 organizations offer seminars, and that American companies have spent some $8 billion for their services in 1985 (Margolis 1987). In Canada, a survey of private business and trade/vocational schools by Statistics Canada in 1986 showed that there were 867 licensed private ventures of that sort. Three quarters of these were private training institutions and over two-thirds of the 3,677 programmes recorded were evenly split between two general fields—'Commerce, management and business administration' and 'Engineering and applied sciences' (Statistics Canada 1988).

Quite clearly, given the trivialization of the process of licensing of such ventures by provincial governments—these programmes are lumped together with dance schools and the like—a large number of private concerns supplying educational services have not bothered to seek a license. So we are dealing with a subset of private suppliers. These licensed private suppliers catered to some 187,600 students in 1986; the majority were regular programmes, but 859 were customized. Close to 90 per cent of these programmes led to diplomas or certificates. The survey revealed that 60 per cent of the schools that operated with a license in 1986 had started up during this decade, i.e., between 1980 and 1986—with all regions showing an upward trend.

To gain a perspective on the structure of supply in this market, we have analyzed a data bank on courses and programmes available in Canada at the Training Information Centre of the Public Service Commission of Canada. This Centre was set up to assist any agency of the federal government seeking standard or customised training programmes or courses. This data bank contains the names of some 283 suppliers. The sample is not randomly generated, since firms or agencies may ask to be listed, and since those asking to be put on the list obviously have an eye to supplying training services to the federal government. But the structure of the private education/training business is somewhat revealed through this snapshot.

There are at present 3490 courses listed as offered in the broad categories of management (3029), finance (306) and material management (155). A simple classification of these courses according to the types of providers shows that the traditional post-secondary institutions—mainly through their extension departments, training centres, etc.—control only half of this market. Informal discussions with those who have constructed this data base indicate that this group of providers has been losing ground in the 1980s. (Table 2)

More recently, governments' direct entry into training and development has paralleled the growth of corporate colleges. Bill C-148 passed on August 25, 1988 in the House of Commons in Ottawa established the Canadian Centre for Management Development in Ottawa—an area already equipped with three universities and two major colleges claiming to serve this market (Canada 1988).

Table 2
Courses in management, finance and material management available in the listing of the Public Service Commission (September 1988)

Suppliers type	No.	Number of courses (e)	(f)	total	%
Consultants, private producers	205	1,041	152	1,193	34.2
University & college based agencies	63	1,542	180	1,722	49.3
Professional associations	3	40	0	40	49.3
Government departments	12	369	166	535	15.3
Total	283	2,992	498	3,490	100.0

Notes:
(e) courses offered in English
(f) en français

The message is clear: on the Canadian scene, albeit more slowly than in the United States, non-traditional production of higher education is growing. The 1980s have seen the expansion of private production of higher education on a scale not experienced up to now. Even the public sector would appear to have developed a growing reliance on the non-traditional providers, and has already pioneered the concept of 'public corporate college'.

This poses new challenges to the traditional stakeholders of the post-secondary enterprise.

Alternative Strategies

In the United States—which today leads the way—'there may well be as many people enroled in corporate programmes as in traditional institutions of higher learning' (Margolis 1987) and the new trend is 'the corporate university—company-sponsored, accredited universities that incorporate the best of the Japanese, European and American experience... IBM does more education and training than Columbia and Princeton combined' (Botkin 1987).

Much of employer-sponsored training and development activities and what was done by corporate colleges has been maligned by traditional educators as not accredited, trivial in content, narrowly vocational, and staffed by a low quality professorate. These attacks are not heard any longer in the United States: reviews of many of these programmes have shown them to be impressive, challenging, staffed by extremely competent and experienced persons, and easily accreditable if and when the opportunity to do so is open.

It would appear that Canada will follow this American trend with a lag but, with the opening of borders created by free trade, it is not unreasonable to conjecture a penetration of private employer-sponsored institutions from the United States that might catalyse the process. The City University of Washington already offers non-traditional programmes in Vancouver; the Master of Science in Manufacturing Management is offered by the General Motors Institute of Michigan on GM premises in Oshawa.

There are many reasons to believe that this trend to employer-sponsored instruction and corporate colleges is here to stay: they have developed a particularly potent mix of specialisation, practical skills and theoretical knowledge in their curriculum, they have much greater flexibility than traditional institutions in adapting to change, in managing human resources and in keeping abreast: their TED mix is cheaper, more current and more flexible than what is available in traditional institutions (Nash/Hawthorne 1987).

Governments may choose two approaches: (1) ignore the problem; (2) treat non-collegiate-sponsored institutions as accredited private institutions and require a special board to overview such institutions.

For the time being, ignoring the problem is the dominant strategy. Governments act in collusion with traditional institutions to deny accreditation to private programmes or schools, at least at the post-secondary level. In this sense, Canadian practice differs significantly both from the American process where there is little attempt to establish a public monopoly on the granting of degrees, and from the United Kingdom where no license or legislative approval is required to grant a degree. In Canada, the granting of authority for awarding degrees is a prerogative of provincial legislatures (Skolnik 1987). As a result, non-traditional approaches to higher education have not developed well in Canada (Skolnik 1986).

At the secondary school level, governments have agreed to license private schools and to allow them to compete with the public institutions. It has been argued that such competition has proved healthy and productive for the public schools. In the case of universities and colleges, the preservation of the public institutions from competition through their public monopoly on the granting of degrees (together with government unwillingness to interfere openly in the management of traditional post-secondary institutions) has amounted to a certain lack of progressiveness. There are signs in many provinces however of a drift toward more willingness to open this market to competition (Skolnik 1987). This might unleash an important growth in private production of higher education in Canada.

As could be expected, traditional institutions attempt to persuade governments to maintain their paradoxical policy: preventing competition from non-traditional agencies, while maintaining a strict non-intervention policy in the affairs of traditional institutions. They argue that any non-traditional component of importance can be enfranchised through co-optation by traditional institutions (indirect accreditation via bilateral arrangements with a traditional institution) or through the extension of the traditional institutions into the domain of the non-traditional (through cooperative programmes, short courses, executive development programmes and better use of extension courses or continuing education units).

This strategy of new alliances between traditional higher-education establishments and the private/public sectors communities will not resolve all problems. It may lead at best to the grafting of non-traditional components at the fringe of traditional institutions through the creation of units only loosely connected with the mainframe of traditional institutions. Such units are bound to remain alien to the main university activities: they will suffer from the inflexibility and slowness of the traditional PSE and often be prevented by the academy to design the very educational services they have been set up to produce. Moreover, the existing staff of traditional post-secondary institutions will prove less capable of handling these new demands than anticipated. One is astounded, for instance, at the extraordinary large proportion of the teaching staff in those peripheral programmes that is drawn from outside the traditional academic community—even at the Executive MBA level.

The recent growth in corporate colleges in the United States, following a period of experimentation with new alliances, confirm these impressions. Corporate-higher education alliances have not worked out. This has been the result of much insensitivity on the part of the guilt-ridden post-secondary institutions (Paquet 1988). What would be required from these institutions is nothing less than a major recasting of their model and regime. This is unlikely to happen organically (Lynton 1984; Newson/Buchbinder 1988; Paquet/von zur Muehlen 1988).

Conclusion

There has been a phenomenal growth in the private production of higher education in Canada. Demand has grown in all sectors and suppliers have emerged to respond to this demand over the last decade. It is only a matter of time before large private concerns in Canada seize upon the opportunity to emulate the Rand Corporation or Arthur D. Little and create true corporate colleges. (Holmes 1981)

There is little doubt that governments will not be allowed to enforce the monopoly of the professional academics in the face of alternative providers that can demonstrate that they can supply educational services more effectively, more efficiently and more cheaply. The experiences of other countries will be used to show that in the higher education sector as in so many others public monopolies may not be the optimal strategy.

Demographics should play a key role in this transformation of the learning enterprise: a switch of consumers to non-traditional instruction and a rapid growth of providers of new and different learning services may be expected. In the 1990s, the biggest cohort of students in higher education will be the age group of 35 and over. This group will call for non-traditional higher education—competent, compact, mixing training/development/education in new creative ways. There is little doubt as to who will capture that market—the traditionalists or the entrepreneurs.

References

Adams, R.J. 1980. 'Training in Canadian Industry: Research, Theory and Policy Implications'. Hamilton: McMaster University, Faculty of Business, Research & Working Paper Series No. 168, April.

Basken R., et al. 1988. *Focus 2000—Report of the Task Force on Harnessing Change*. Ottawa, Montréal, Toronto: The Canadian Chamber of Commerce.

Botkin, J. 1987. 'Balancing the Education Equation'. *World.* July.

Canada. 1988. *Bill C-148—An Act to Establish the Canadian Centre for Management Development and to Amend Certain Acts in Consequence Thereof.* Ottawa: House of Commons, August 25.

Carnavale, A.P. 1986. 'The Learning Enterprise'. *Training & Development Journal.* 40, 1, January.

Conseil de la science et de la technologie du Québec. 1985. *Les sciences sociales et humaines et l'entreprise privée.* (mimeo 27p).

Employment & Immigration. 1987. 'Aperçu des résultats d'une enquête sur la formation dans l'industrie'. *Bulletin du marché du travail.* 4, 2, Mars.

Eurich, N.P. 1985. *Corporate Classrooms—The Learning Business.* Princeton: The Carnegie Foundation for the Advancement of Teaching.

Gunderson, M. 1978. 'Training in Canada: Progress and Problems'. In Government Involvement in Training, ed. by B.O. Pettman. Bradford: MCB Publications.

Hirsch, E.D. Jr. 1988. *Cultural Literacy.* New York: Vintage Books.

Holmes, J. 1981. 'What is the Future of Corporate Education in Canada?' (mimeo 17p.)

Labour Canada. 1979. *Education and Working Canadians—Report of the Commission of Inquiry on Educational Leave and Productivity.* Ottawa.

Leblanc, F.E., et al. 1987. *Federal Policy on Post-Secondary Education.* Report of the Standing Senate Committee on National Finance, Second Session, Thirty-third Parliament. Ottawa: Supply & Services.

Lusterman, S. 1985. *Trends in Corporate Education and Training.* New York: The Conference Board, Report No. 870.

Lynton, E.A. 1984. *The Missing Connection between Business and the Universities.* New York: Collier Macmillan Publishers.

Margolis, S.J. 1987. 'Of Classrooms . . . and Boardrooms'. *World.* July.

Nash, N.S. and E.M. Hawthorne. 1987. *Formal Recognition of Employer-Sponsored Instruction: Conflict and Collegiality in Post-secondary Education.* Washington, D.C., College Station, Texas: Clearinghouse on Higher Education, Association for the Study of Higher Education.

National Forum on Post-Secondary Education. 1987. *The Forum Papers.* Halifax, N.S.: The Institute for Research on Public Policy.

Newson, J. and H. Buchbinder. 1988. *The University Means Business.* Toronto: Garamond Press.

Olson, L. 1986. 'Training Trends: The Corporate View'. *Training & Development Journal.* 40, 9, September.

Paquet, G. 1988. 'Two Tramps in Mud Time or The Social Sciences and Humanities in Modern Society'. In *The Human Sciences*, ed. by B. Abu-Laban, B.G. Rule. Edmonton: The University of Alberta Press.

Paquet, G. 1989. 'Liberal Education as Synecdoche'. In *Who's Afraid of Liberal Education?* C. Andrew et al. Ottawa: Social Sciences Federation of Canada (in press).

Paquet, G. and M. Von Zur-Muehlen. 1988. *Education Canada?— Higher Education on the Brink.* Ottawa: Canadian Higher Education Research Network, (2nd Ed.).

Peterfreund, S. 1976. 'Education in Industry—Today and in the Future'. *Training and Development Journal.* 30, 5, May.

Reeves, L.H. 1983. *Formateur d'adultes: une profession naissante et nécessaire.* Ottawa: Employment & Immigration Canada, Document d'information 30.

Skolnik, M.L. 1986. 'Diversity in Higher Education: The Canadian Case'. *Higher Education in Europe.* I, 2.

Skolnik, M.L. 1987. 'State Control of Degree Granting: The Establishment of a Public Monopoly in Canada'. In *Governments and Higher Education—The Legitimacy of Intervention*, ed. by C. Watson. Toronto: The Ontario Institute for Studies in Education.

Statistics Canada. 1988. *Education Statistics Bulletin.* 10, 4 May.

Toulmin, S. 1988. 'The Recovery of Practical Philosophy'. *The American Scholar.* 57, 3.

Wilcox, J. 1987. 'A Campus Tour of Corporate Colleges'. *Training & Development Journal.* 41, 5, May.

VI

LLOYDS BANK LECTURE

Education for Life and Work in the 1990s

SIR JEREMY MORSE
   CHAIRMAN OF LLOYDS BANK PLC
   PRESIDENT OF THE BRITISH BANKERS' ASSOCIATION

I have been delighted to attend part of this Canada-UK Colloquium on education, and I am honoured to be asked to round it off with a Lloyds Bank lecture. Thirty-five years ago I was eager to move on from university to the commercial world. Recently I have been reminded how crucially important good education is for the functioning of our modern societies, and I have renewed my involvement with it. Obviously I am no expert in it, not even in British education, but I would like to make it the subject of my remarks.

Education is certainly a topical subject in many countries—which is a pleasant surprise since public attention is not often focussed on what is really important for the longer term. No doubt this topicality springs mainly from dissatisfaction with education systems and the preparation they have provided for later life and work in the 1980s. But before we discuss the present situation and what needs to be altered, we should look forward to see what the 1990s will be like.

This must be done broadly. Any attempt at precise forward planning runs too big a risk of misdirection, particularly in education. How many educationalists foresaw twenty years ago the present development of screen and keyboard? The children beginning school today will have their working lives in another millennium. Nevertheless, a forward look is a sensible cross-check on our present convictions.

At the broadest level, the world is likely to continue to become more plural, with no unifying ideology, no dominant country and increasing intercommunication and interdependence. Populations will still be growing in most countries. Larger populations mean an increased need to operate by teamwork, and education can enhance the role of each member of the team. So there is a goal for everyone—a message which education must instill, at the same time as it develops excellence and shapes round pegs for round holes.

The advance of automation will affect the character of the teamwork we need in more than one way. Now that the computer is becoming a personal tool, the use and handling of computerised machines and instruments will become an essential part of daily life and communication. They will do away with monotonous repetitive work on assembly lines, just as they will free brainpower from bookkeeping and shorthand typing. One of the most exciting things on the horizon is the end of two centuries of forms of mass production in which men and women have often become slaves of the machine, with countless social and moral consequences, most of them deleterious.

But this refound freedom and mastery of our new tools will still further increase competitive pressures and keep the pace of change going, putting a high premium for both society and individuals on adaptability and the transfer of skills. Both pre-industrial and industrial societies had their routines, which may have been limiting, but which gave life a rhythm. Post-industrial society will have to find new rhythms, either of more changeful work or of mixed work and leisure.

Population growth and technological advance are secular trends. Economic and political developments are more cyclical. Nevertheless it seems likely that the current trend away from government controls towards the freer play of market forces has many years yet to run. If so, this will be a further force for change and competition.

Nor can we expect stability in the international monetary system. The net debtor position of the United States is already half a trillion dollars, and this will rise to 1-$1\frac{1}{2}$ trillion dollars in the 1990s. This will cause few problems when there is confidence in the United States economy and currency: individuals and institutions will pat their stuffed wallets and think of their dollars as money. But periodically there will be losses of confidence, when holders will be trying to get out of the big tank of the dollar into the smaller tanks of the yen or the mark or the pound or gold. This will produce big fluctuations in exchange rates and consequently in interest rates, and prevent the re-establishment of a general system of fixed exchange rates.

Whenever the United States economy slows down, the maintenance of world growth will depend on the other major economies. Hence the perceived need for Japan and Europe to promote domestic growth, relying less on exports to the United States, and to develop trade and capital flows between themselves. It used to be said that when America sneezes the rest of the world catches pneumonia. Given the size of their combined economies, now larger than that of the United States, Japan and the European Community are beginning to realise that this is no longer necessarily the case and are correspondingly gaining self-confidence. Nor is this picture of sustainable if moderate growth seriously threatened by a return to galloping inflation. Although inflation has not been completely exorcised, and although the United States, as a major debtor, may become somewhat less hostile to it, bad memories of 1973-1982 should serve to keep it in check.

Evidently there is a trend towards economic blocs, particularly for the OECD countries. The most obvious example is the European Community, where the movement towards integration is reinforced by a political thread. In addition to the twelve member countries, this grouping attracts the five remaining EFTA countries. On this side of the Atlantic we have the proposed free trade area between the United States and Canada, which if successfully established could be extended to Mexico and beyond. A Far Eastern economic zone is forming around Japan, which will help to reduce the excessive interdependence between the United States and Japan. And there are closer economic relations between Australia and New Zealand. Only in the Communist bloc are there signs of political and economic disintegration, while the countries of the developing world are generally still too oppressed by debt and other problems to be able to combine effectively.

There is a good chance that these blocs of the 1990s will be more benign—i.e., less hostile and less protectionist towards one another—than in the 1930s, mainly because the intercommunication and interdependence to which I have already referred are global rather than regional. This should help us to avoid a third world war, in which case the human race's penchant for conflict will continue to show itself in local wars, internal dissension and terrorism.

If this is the sort of world we are facing, what are the current trends in education and are they the right ones? Inevitably my answers to these questions will mainly reflect British experience, although I believe that they could also stand for a number of other countries.

One trend is a renewed emphasis on communication skills, not only the traditional 'three Rs' of reading, writing and arithmetic with their basic elements of grammar and numeracy, but oral skills and the modern skills of screen and keyboard. This emphasis must be right. All walks of life require a supply of new entrants equipped with these basic skills. Indeed they become more necessary as we move away from mass production. In former times a farm or factory hand without these communication skills could still pick up the work by copying others in the line. Not so now. Jobs have become separated and specialized, and the new recruit has almost from the beginning to be able to understand instructions and to report back. In such conditions the use of screen and keyboard will prove to be a fundamental means of communication like pen and ink, and not an optional extra like a typewriter.

However, it is important not to confuse these basis skills with the subjects in which they most naturally reside, i.e., the native language and mathematics. Certainly that is where the acquisition of these skills starts, but reading and writing can be improved by going on to other languages and other humane subjects, and arithmetic can be extended by going on to the sciences and to technical subjects like engineering. Indeed the evidence suggests that these skills are most thoroughly inculcated if they are insisted on throughout the curriculum, e.g., if science teachers insist on well-written reports, historians insist on accurate quantification, etc.

There are two other reasons why it is unwise to align basic skills too narrowly with subjects, as some traditionalists tend to do. At one end of the spectrum of ability you make life more difficult than it will be anyway for the less clever or less intellectual child, increasing the bias against manual skills which is ingrained in modern society. At the other end, you work against the second main current trend in educational reform, which is a move away from excessive specialisation towards a broader curriculum and awareness of the inter-relations between different subjects. This is particularly needed in Britain where we push 16-year-olds who are staying in education to narrow their focus to only three subjects, which may themselves be closely related (e.g., physics, chemistry and mathematics, or English, French and Spanish).

The reform of education in Britain is just bringing in a new examination at 16 for a General Certificate of Secondary Education (GCSE), replacing the former O-level examination. Unavoidably perhaps, the change-over is confused and confusing for many of the children, parents and teachers immediately involved. But the broadening trend which underlies it is evident. More emphasis is laid on acquiring skills and less on rote knowledge. Children are required to do projects as well as exams, and assessment as well as exam results goes into their gradings. There is more scope for inter-disciplinary or bridge subjects, of which modern geography is a good example. This is a much broader and more demanding subject than it was in my school days. It is also more rewarding than sociology, another inter-disciplinary subject, perhaps because it is closer to the natural sciences and more numerate.

Just as the renewed emphasis on basic communication skills is highly appropriate for the 1990s, so is this broadening trend. If there is going to be more change, people will need to be more adaptable and more self-reliant. Everybody who goes on to higher education, but does not stay on in academic life has to be able not only to carry their basic skills through and out into the world, but also to transfer the more advanced skills that higher education has given them (whether they are specific to their chosen subjects or more general skills like logical thinking, scientific method, understanding of systems) and apply them to non-academic life and work. This transfer will surely be facilitated if we can avoid too narrow an academic focus right up to university graduation.

I would like to hope that not only the content, but also the flavour of education could be changed in the same direction of encouraging adaptability and self-reliance. Most people naturally dislike change, particularly if imposed from outside, and the more so as they get older. Our present educational system does little to redress this. All too often education seems like a conveyor belt along which one travels, and which—provided one passed a number of checkpoints—will eventually deliver one into a job which may itself be another longer conveyor belt. Whereas, if pupils and students have to make more choices and decisions for themselves in the course of their education, they may subsequently accept more easily that change is part of life, and not something arbitrarily imposed on them, and may be readier to see opportunities for themselves in such change.

If these trends are in the right direction, who will see that they are developed and carried through to a good conclusion? If I am right in predicting that the movement away from government control towards a freer market will persist through the 1990s, then both the governmental contribution and the governmental influence will decline. At the moment the British government is seeking to extend its influence as it puts up less money, but there is a limit to this, since he who pays the piper will sooner or later call the tune. There is a view that parent power will fill whatever vacuum the government may leave, but desirable as this might be it is unlikely to develop in practice.

This brings me to my own particular interest as a businessman. I am sure that good education will be an even more important condition for economic success—at the personal, corporate, national and global level—in the future than it has been in the past. As I have already argued, individuals have to learn to be more adaptable, companies have to learn to work more as teams, nations have to learn how to maintain productivity in unstable conditions and the world has to learn how to cope with the tensions created by growing interdependence. So although I do not regard economic success as the be-all and end-all of life, let alone of education, there is plenty to be done on this aspect of education in most of our countries before we need start worrying about whether we are overdoing it.

In the past year I was a member of a Task Force set up in Britain by the Confederation of British Industry to consider these questions in relating to secondary education. Its main conclusions were:

1. We need a better mutual understanding by business and education of what each should expect of the other.

2. Business cannot afford to stand aside from the educational debate, if it is to get the workforce it needs for the future.

3. The key to success is the establishment of local links between particular businesses and particular schools. These links can take many forms, e.g., pupil and teacher work shadowing, work experience and secondments, problem solving projects, careers guidance, curriculum development, businessmen becoming governors, and compacts (whereby employers agree with schools that they will take on pupils who have met certain standards).

4. Local links need to be backed up by appropriate organizations within companies and at regional and national level. In Britain at present there is a confusing 'alphabet soup' of initiatives by the private sector as well as by different arms of Government.

But education is not something that ends when children leave school, and more emphasis on training will be needed from employers in the future. Relevant points in this regard are:

1. Business regularly offers relatively high wages to attract 16-year olds into employment without giving them much training. Such a short-sighted approach does little to promote confidence among teachers that British business takes training seriously. In Japan 95 per cent of children stay on after 16 in full-time education. Germany has a widespread system of apprentice training at work coupled with day release. Too many 16-year-olds in Britain do neither, although the recent Youth Training Scheme points in a better direction.

2. Britain (like many other countries) faces a demographic time bomb, with the number of 16-17 year olds falling by one-quarter between 1968 and 1994. This will increase competition for school-leavers. So the turnover of junior staff will need to be

reduced by offering training and job enrichment, as well as changing payment systems.

3. Existing staff need training too, so that they are able to take on new jobs. Giving older people these new skills will be more difficult and more expensive.

4. The decline of the traditional apprentice system needs to be reversed and the model extended from its traditional base in manual crafts to the new technologies and to serve businesses.

These thoughts should present no problems to polytechnics, but I have some concern as to how they might be extended to university education. If schools can improve the education of their pupils for life and work, and if businessmen and other employers can improve their recruitment and training programmes to put school-leavers quickly and happily to work, will universities assist or interrupt this process? How will they successfully achieve their triple task of supplying one stream of graduates to academic research, another stream to the teaching profession and a third stream more readily than their teachers? It is certainly encouraging to see the growth in recent years of undergraduate-led industrial societies in British universities.

The differing experiences of Britain and Japan are perhaps instructive. Britain produces far more than its fair share of Nobel prize winners, but has a relatively low level of general education. Japan is the opposite on both points. Surprisingly, both countries are trying to change in the direction of the other. It may simply be that there is an ideal *via media* to be sought, but to me it suggests that one country cannot excel at both ends of the scale. Countries, like pupils, have to learn to make choices. I have no doubt that education, at least in many Western countries, needs to be more closely related to life and work, and that this is a task in which the teaching profession, government and business must cooperate.